# Application Management

 **ITIL**® Managing IT services

Office of Government Commerce

*London*: TSO

Published by TSO (The Stationery Office) and available from:

**Online**
**www.tso.co.uk/bookshop**

**Mail, Telephone, Fax & E-mail**
TSO
PO Box 29, Norwich, NR3 1GN
Telephone orders/General enquiries: 0870 600 5522
Fax orders: 0870 600 5533
E-mail: book.orders@tso.co.uk
Textphone 0870 240 3701

**TSO Shops**
123 Kingsway, London, WC2B 6PQ
020 7242 6393 Fax 020 7242 6394
68-69 Bull Street, Birmingham B4 6AD
0121 236 9696 Fax 0121 236 9699
9-21 Princess Street, Manchester M60 8AS
0161 834 7201 Fax 0161 833 0634
16 Arthur Street, Belfast BT1 4GD
028 9023 8451 Fax 028 9023 5401
18-19 High Street, Cardiff CF10 1PT
029 2039 5548 Fax 029 2038 4347
71 Lothian Road, Edinburgh EH3 9AZ
0870 606 5566 Fax 0870 606 5588

**TSO Accredited Agents**
(see Yellow Pages)

*and through good booksellers*

For further information on OGC products, contact:

OGC Service Desk
Rosebery Court
St Andrews Business Park
Norwich NR7 0HS
Telephone +44 (0) 845 000 4999

Published for the Office of Government Commerce under licence from the
Controller of Her Majesty's Stationery Office

© Crown Copyright 2002

This is a Value Added product which is outside the scope of the HMSO Click Use Licence.

Applications to reuse, reproduce or republish material in this publication should be sent to HMSO, Licensing Division,
St Clements House, 2-16 Colegate, Norwich, NR3 1BQ, Tel No. (01603) 621000 Fax No. (01603) 723000, E-mail: hmsolicensing@cabinet-office.x.gsi.gov.uk, or
complete the application form on the HMSO website www.hmso.gov.uk/forms/cform2.htm
HMSO, in consultation with Office of Government Commerce (OGC) will prepare a licence based on standard terms tailored to your particular requirements
including payment terms

First published 2002
Second impression 2003

ISBN 0 11 330866 3

Printed in the United Kingdom for The Stationery Office.

c3    02/03    108062    810537

Titles within the ITIL series include:

**Service Support (Published 2000)**
Service Desk and the Process of Incident
Management, Problem Management, Configuration
Management, Change Management and
Release Management                    ISBN 0 11 330015 8

**Service Delivery (Published 2001)**
Capacity Management, Availability Management,
Service Level Management, IT Service Continuity,
Financial Management for IT Services and
Customer Relationship Management      ISBN 0 11 330017 4

**Planning to Implement Service Management (Published 2002)**    ISBN 0 11 330877 9
**ICT Infrastructure Management (Published 2002)**    ISBN 0 11 330865 5
**Security Management**    ISBN 0 11 330014 X

ITIL back catalogue – an historical repository available as PDF downloads from www.tso.co.uk/ITIL

The managers' set
The complementary guidance set
Environmental management, strategy and computer operations set

# CONTENTS

## FOREWORD

Organisations are increasingly dependent on electronic delivery of services to meet Customer needs. This means a requirement for high quality IT services, matched to business needs and User requirements as they evolve.

OGC's ITIL (IT Infrastructure Library) is the most widely accepted approach to IT Service Management in the world. ITIL provides a cohesive set of best practice, drawn from the public and private sectors internationally, supported by a comprehensive qualification scheme, accredited training organisations, implementation and assessment tools.

Bob Assirati

OGC

## PREFACE

The ethos behind the development of ITIL (IT Infrastructure Library) is the recognition that organisations are increasingly dependent upon IT to satisfy their corporate aims and meet their business needs. This growing dependency leads to growing needs for quality IT services – quality that is matched to business needs and User requirements as they emerge.

This is true no matter what type or size of organisation, be it national government, a multinational conglomerate, a decentralised office with either a local or centralised IT provision, an outsourced Service Provider, or a single office environment with one person providing IT support. In each case there is the requirement to provide an economical service that is reliable, consistent and fit for purpose.

IT Service Management is concerned with delivering and supporting IT services that are appropriate to the business requirements of the organisation. ITIL provides a comprehensive, consistent and coherent set of best practices for IT Service Management processes, promoting a quality approach to achieving business effectiveness and efficiency in the use of information systems. ITIL Service Management processes are intended to be implemented so that they underpin but do not dictate the business processes of an organisation. IT Service Providers will be striving to improve the quality of the service, but at the same time they will be trying to reduce the costs or, at a minimum, maintain costs at the current level.

The best-practice processes promoted in this book both support and are supported by the British Standards Institution's Standard for IT Service Management (BS15000), and the ISO quality standard ISO9000.

## The authors

The guidance in this book was distilled from the experience of a range of authors working in the private sector in IT Service Management. The material was written by:

| | |
|---|---|
| Anthony Baron | Microsoft – UK |
| Bret Clarke | Microsoft – USA |
| Paul Hertroys | IBM – The Netherlands |
| Norbert van Oosterom | IBM – The Netherlands |

with contributions from:

| | |
|---|---|
| David Hinley | DS Hinley Associates |

The project was managed and coordinated by Paul Hertroys of IBM Netherlands.

A wide-ranging national and international Quality Assurance (QA) exercise was carried out by people proposed by OGC and *it*SMF. OGC and IBM wish to express their particular appreciation to the following people who spent considerable time and effort (far beyond the call of duty!) on QA of the material:

| | |
|---|---|
| David Bainbridge | DMR Consulting Pty Ltd (Canada) |
| Craig Bates | Proactive Services Pty Ltd |
| Dave Bingham | Fujitsu Consulting |
| Karen Cughan | DMR Consulting Pty Ltd (Canada) |

Michael Davies      Proactive Services Pty Ltd
Catherine Davis      DMR Consulting Pty Ltd
Stephen Eates      DMR Consulting Pty Ltd (Canada)
Jon Hirst      DMR Consulting Pty Ltd
Sjoerd Hulzinger      PinkRoccade (NL)
Tony Jenkins      Parity
Kari Johnson
Chris Jones      Independent Consulting – Australia
Sue Morris      PinkRoccade (NL)
Tuomas Nurmela      Sonera
Remco van der Polse      PinkRoccade (NL)
Chris Poynter      DMR Consulting Pty Ltd
Glen Purdy      DMR Consulting Pty Ltd
Colin Rudd      IT Enterprise Management Services
Don Sinden      Fujitsu Consulting
Sid Stephen      Vice President, Application Outsourcing, Fujitsu Consulting
Keith Tarran
Paul Turner
Paul Wilkinson      PinkRoccade (NL)
Rob van Winden      Red Dolphin ICT Services

## Contact information

Full details of the range of material published under the ITIL banner can be found at www.itil.co.uk

For further information on this and other OGC products, please visit the OGC website at www.ogc.gov.uk

Alternatively, please contact:

OGC Service Desk
Rosebery Court
St Andrews Business Park
Norwich
NR7 0HS
United Kingdom
Tel: +44 (0) 845 000 4999
E-mail: ServiceDesk@ogc.gsi.gov.uk

# █ INTRODUCTION

## 1.1    The structure of ITIL

This book is one of a series issued as part of the ITIL framework that documents industry best practice for IT Service Management. Originally developed in the late 1980s, ITIL has evolved and been updated to address the modern challenges offered by distributed computing, the Internet, and the need for tighter integration of IT with business operations and objectives. The concept of managing IT services for the improvement of business functions is not new: it predates ITIL. The idea of bringing the entire Service Management best practice together under one roof was, however, both radical and new.

Figure 1.1 shows each of the ITIL books with the Service Management processes at the heart of the framework.

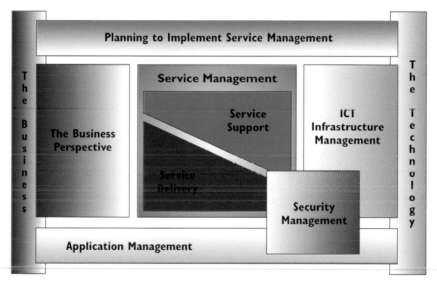

*Figure 1.1 – The ITIL publication framework*

### 1.1.1    The Business Perspective

*The Business Perspective* aims to familiarise business management with the underlying components and architecture design of the Information and Communications Technology (ICT) infrastructure necessary to support their business processes and gain an understanding of Service Management standards and better practice.

*The Business Perspective* helps the business to understand the benefits of best practice in IT Service Management, while at the same time helping the Service Provider to talk on level terms with the business. Similarly, *Planning to Implement Service Management* helps Service Providers plan their implementation of Service Management best practice while at the same time helping the business to talk on level terms with the Service Provider.

### 1.1.2    ICT Infrastructure Management

*ICT Infrastructure Management* covers all aspects of ICT infrastructure management from identification of business requirements through the tendering process, to the testing, installation, deployment and ongoing support and maintenance of the ICT components and IT services. The book describes the major processes involved in the management of all areas and aspects of technology and includes:

- ■ Design and Planning processes
- ■ Deployment processes
- ■ Operations processes
- ■ Technical Support processes.

### 1.1.3    Service Support

The ITIL processes covered in the *Service Support* book are depicted in Figure 1.2:

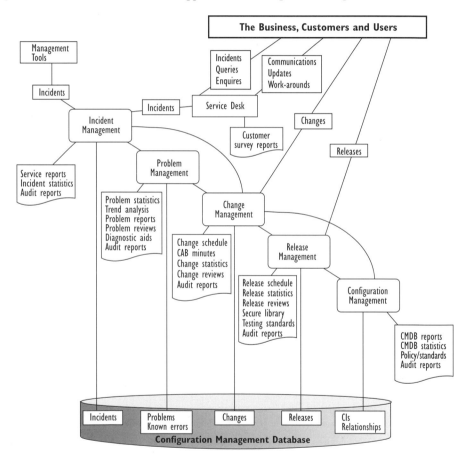

*Figure 1.2 – Service Support: coverage*

### 1.1.4 Service Delivery

The ITIL processes covered in the *Service Delivery* book are depicted in Figure 1.3:

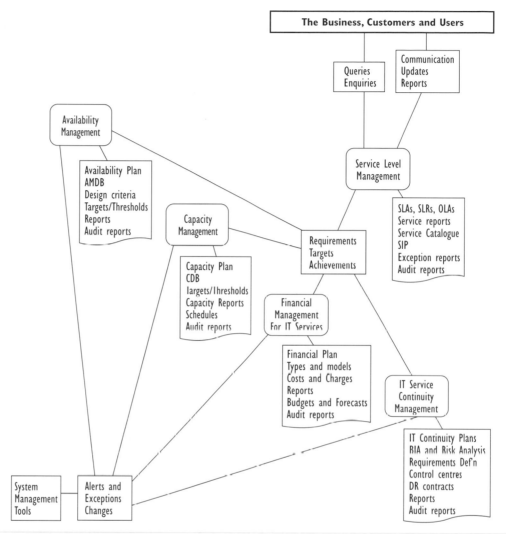

*Figure 1.3 – Service Delivery: coverage*

## 1.1.5 Planning to Implement Service Management

The *Planning to Implement* book focuses on key issues to be considered when planning the implementation of IT Service Management. The steps required to implement or improve IT service provision are explained, and guidance is provided on the alignment of business needs to IT, enabling an assessment of whether IT service provision is really meeting the needs of the business. *Planning to Implement Service Management* gives practical guidance on the evaluation of the current maturity levels of Service Management and on implementing the processes involved.

## 1.1.6 Application Management

The last piece of the ITIL framework deals with Application Management, which is the subject of this book. *Application Management* addresses the complex subject of managing applications from the initial business need, through the Application Management lifecycle, up to and including retirement. In addition, *Application Management* includes the interaction with IT

Service Management disciplines contained in *Service Delivery, Service Support* and *ICT Infrastructure Management*. This book places a strong emphasis on ensuring that IT projects and strategies are tightly aligned with those of the business throughout the applications lifecycle. This is critically important in ensuring that the business is receiving, and IT is delivering, the proper value for the investments made.

For the purposes of this book, an application is defined as the software program(s) that perform those specific functions that directly support the execution of business functions, processes, and/or procedures. Applications, along with data and infrastructure components, such as hardware, the operating system, and middleware, make up the technology components of IT systems that in turn are part of an IT service. This is all explained in detail within the chapters of this book.

The major elements of ITIL, as illustrated in the overlapping pieces of Figure 1.1, are somewhat analogous to the tectonic plates that make up our planet. Each has elements that have a precise fit, and some that overlap or do not fit together precisely. At the highest level, there are no strict demarcation lines. Indeed, the analogy of tectonic plates, sliding over and under one another, joining and separating, and creating points of instability, applies well to ITIL. It is precisely where process domains overlap or where demarcation lines cannot be clearly drawn that many management problems arise. No one can prevent all the problems occurring (just as no one can prevent an earthquake), but advice can be provided on how to prepare for and deal with them.

## 1.2   Defining the problem

There are many challenges faced by businesses in today's modern digital world of information. The demand that businesses respond rapidly to changes in market conditions and that their IT organisations support and, in many cases, enable these changes, is very real. These challenges create many problems for the IT professional, not least of which is how to effectively manage the applications that are necessary to move the business forward. The use of information technology is increasingly rapidly, and the simple fact that applications house the majority of business functionality demands that they be managed like the corporate assets they are. The situation is further complicated by the fact that, because of the emergence of e-business, Customers deal directly with the information technology of the company they are dealing with. This puts extra pressure on the reliability and scalability of the information technology employed. Redundant system functionality, poorly aligned objectives, lengthy deployment schedules, poor systems availability, and reliability are all issues that must be addressed within Application Management.

A key issue that has existed for some time is the problem of moving application developers and IT Service Management closer together. The lack of Service Management considerations within *all* phases of the application lifecycle has been a serious deficiency for some time. Applications should be deployed with Service Management requirements included. They should be designed and built for operability, reliability, performance and manageability, tested for compliance and so on. The importance of this problem can be highlighted by the Gartner Group report which showed that nearly 80% of production outages occur as a result of operator error (40%) and application failures (40%). The remaining 20% are a result of technology errors caused by the operating system and hardware. Figure 1.4 illustrates this study:

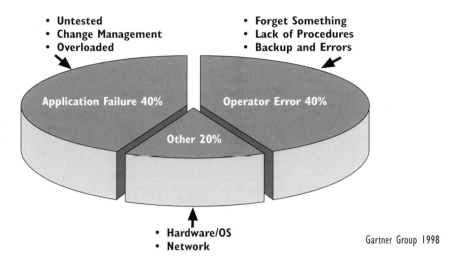

*Figure 1.4 – Production outages*

These statistics clearly show the need for having Application Management and IT Service Management work closely together to reduce the production outages of IT systems.

## 1.3 Objective

Simply stated, the primary objective of this book is to provide sound best practice and practical guidance in Application Management from a Service Management perspective. This approach is taken throughout the book, and all major Application Management topics are covered with Service Management in mind. It is hoped that this approach will be equally valuable to individuals throughout an organisation, including both the business's decision makers (and their representatives) and IT professionals. The historical practice of separating business from Application Management and Application Management from IT Service Management must be discarded. The only way that the production outages described above can be avoided is to have Application Management and Service Management deliver business functionality together throughout every stage of the lifecycle.

In addition, having IT and the business jointly develop their strategies as a mutual effort, should be a precursor to beginning any application development or deployment project. This helps to ensure that IT and the business agree to objectives that are clear, concise, and achievable. Without this all-important first step, the business functionality provided will miss the target and not provide the Return on Investment expected.

## 1.4 Target audience

The target audience for this book is broad and encompasses a wide range of IT professions including:

- IT Service Management
- Information and Communications Technology (ICT) infrastructure management
- technical support

- application development and maintenance
- business development and analysis
- business and IT stakeholders.

However, this book is relevant to virtually anyone who provides IT services to Customers, partners, suppliers, or internal colleagues. It takes a purposely broad perspective and covers many relevant topics, albeit at a more cursory level, as it would be impossible to cover such a complex set of topics in detail within the bounds of one book.

## 1.5 Reading guidance

This book is structured to take the reader through a logical progression, beginning with managing the business value of applications, and determining key business drivers that apply throughout the Application Management lifecycle. The business value section addresses the macro-level of Application Management, which includes managing an entire suite of applications through the use of an application portfolio. From there the book moves to a discussion of delivery strategy options that could be used in the deployment of an application or applications to satisfy the key business drivers. This is followed by a walk-through of an Application Management lifecycle.

In addition, there are chapters covering roles and responsibilities, including team goals and metrics, and Knowledge Management techniques to aid productivity.

The final chapters concern control methods and techniques to ensure that the alignment of key business drivers and the IT systems that enable them is maintained throughout the lifecycle.

This book does not cover application development practices nor address project management and business management issues in detail. These issues are covered in other OGC guidance, such as *Managing Successful Projects with PRINCE2* and the IS Management Guides series. Readers looking for best practices in Rapid Application Development (RAD), Rational Unified Process (RUP) or other development practices will not find any information satisfying their needs. Although business and project management are areas strongly related to applications and Application Management, these management disciplines are regarded as beyond the scope of this book. Some issues related to these topics, such as business and IT alignment and the organisation of roles and functions, are addressed. However, these issues are addressed in relation to the management of applications as corporate assets throughout their lifecycle. This also applies to application development methods and techniques. The influence of these techniques on the application lifecycle is addressed, but best practices in this area are considered beyond the scope of this book.

# 2 POSITIONING OF APPLICATION MANAGEMENT

To fully understand Application Management, it is necessary to contrast it with Service Management and application development.

- **Application Management** is the superset, which describes the overall handling, or management, of the application as it goes through its entire lifecycle. This lifecycle encompasses both the application development phases and Service Management activities noted below. By bringing these two disciplines together, the goals of IT Service Management will be accomplished more easily through the delivery of applications that are more operable and manageable. This is fully described in Chapter 5 of this book, *The Application Management Lifecycle.*

- **Application development** is concerned with the activities needed to plan, design, and build an application that will ultimately be used by some part of the organisation to address a business requirement. This includes application acquisition through custom development, purchase, hosting, provisioning and any combination thereof. It is not concerned with the deployment or ongoing daily management of the application.

- **Service Management** focuses on the activities that are involved with the deployment, operation, support, and optimisation of the application. The main objective is to ensure that the application, once built and deployed, can meet the Service Level that has been defined for it.

Figure 2.1 illustrates the relationships between application development, Service Management, and Application Management.

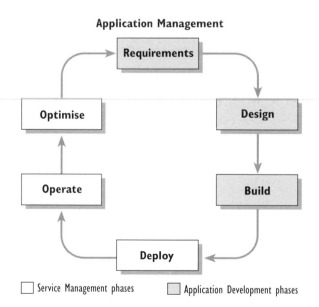

*Figure 2.1 – Relationships between application development, Service Management and Application Management*

Application Management provides a comprehensive, end-to-end description of all the management processes that need to be followed within the lifetime of an application (from conception to retirement). It provides a holistic description of what needs to be done and by whom. Application Management also establishes a road map that all IT professionals can follow to successfully deliver new and existing applications into the IT environment in a more sustainable manner.

Although application development, Service Management, and Application Management are treated here as distinct disciplines, in reality these disciplines are intertwined. The level of integration between the different disciplines is dependent on several factors. These factors can range from the market the organisation is in (e.g. banks have a different approach towards Application Management from that of technology companies), to the standards and guidelines chosen by the organisation.

# 3  MANAGING THE BUSINESS VALUE

## 3.1  Aligning business and IT

### 3.1.1  Understanding the need for aligning business and IT

**'It is not technology itself that supplies returns to a business, but how technology is employed to meet business requirements.'**

The above point, validated by research and documented in a study by IBM and *The Economist* magazine, highlights the need for IT managers to focus more on business requirements and less on specific technology. Doing so will allow the IT manager to employ enabling technology that truly satisfies genuine business need. This, in turn, will result in a much higher rate of return from technology investments because they are enabling business-critical functionality. The benefits of aligning business and IT apply especially well to applications. Applications house the majority of deployed business functionality, making it essential that the business–IT alignment be accurately reflected within the applications employed to ensure that business needs are being satisfied. Without this essential alignment, the risk greatly increases that an organisation will employ applications, and thus business functionality, that do not adequately meet business needs.

Specifically, each company employs applications to achieve certain business objectives. These business objectives are often directed toward serving customers better or executing certain business processes more efficiently. Emerging technologies, such as the Internet, intranet, broadband, wireless, portals and messaging, have resulted in deployments of market-places, business-to-business portals, and business-to-consumer websites that are targeted at servicing customers better. Examples of applications that enable a business process to be executed more efficiently include the enterprise resource planning (ERP) packages, and financial systems, such as accounting, general ledger and invoicing. All the benefits derived are a direct result of aligning business needs and opportunities with enabling technologies and capabilities.

One of the biggest challenges for IT in today's rapidly changing business environment is in accurately aligning IT projects with well-understood business objectives. In many cases, the IT projects themselves are ill-conceived and/or the business objectives are poorly understood. In fact, it is not at all uncommon for an organisation to launch an IT project simply to deploy a new technology because a competitor, or a recognised market leader, has done the same. This might result in deploying a popular technology with little or no concrete business value for the deploying company. A worst case scenario would be that the company's image and customer satisfaction is adversely affected by badly employed technology.

So how do organisations avoid this situation and gain the maximum benefit from their IT investments? Clearly defined business objectives must be aligned with the IT employed. Unfortunately, this is much easier said than done. Before organisations can derive business objectives, they must first identify business functions across the entire domain of the business under consideration. In order to accomplish this, they need to categorise business functions into business areas. This will allow the business owners and IT Service Providers to quickly group business functionality into functional areas, which in turn facilitates the task of mapping IT services and applications against them. This by itself does not complete the business-to-IT alignment needed, but is an excellent starting point for the work of clearly defining business objectives and supporting IT services and applications.

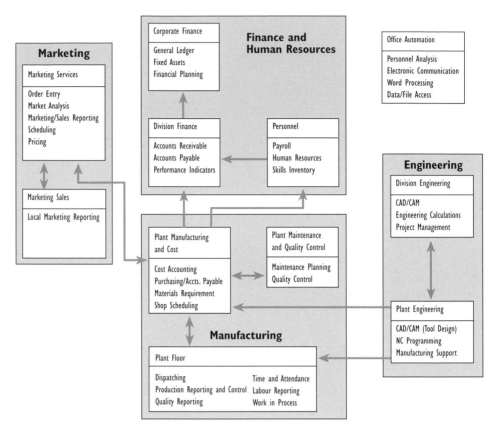

*Figure 3.1 – Example of a high-level business architecture*

Figure 3.1 provides a summary of the major business areas supported for a hypothetical manufacturing company – sales and marketing, engineering, finance, human resources, and manufacturing. Within each of these business areas, the key business functions performed are listed, including, for example, order entry, accounts receivable, CAD/CAM, and dispatching. This listing provides the basis on which to begin the definition of business objectives in each functional area, to be followed by the mapping of IT services and applications against these business objectives. This process is discussed in detail in the following sections of this chapter.

### 3.1.2    A strategic model for business and IT alignment

Henderson and Venkatraman of Harvard University developed a strategic business–IT alignment model (SAM) which provides a structured mechanism for beginning the thought process of marrying business and IT strategies. Just as there are many different business functions performed by a company, there are also many different IT functions that support them. To have a successful alignment, one must consider the multiple perspectives of both the business and IT. The model, which is illustrated in Figure 3.2, attempts to highlight the different perspectives of both sides, and show how these perspectives must be aligned to be successful.

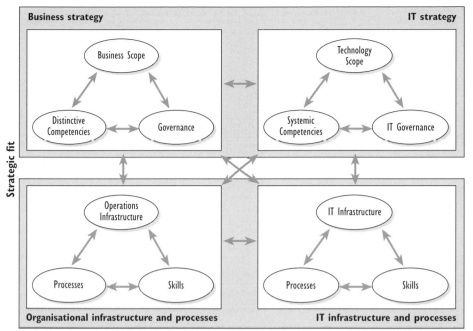

*Figure 3.2 – The strategic alignment model*

This strategic alignment model is based on two building blocks: strategic fit and functional integration. The strategic fit recognises the need to address both the external and internal domain. The external domain is the market in which a company competes, while the internal domain is concerned with the business or IT operations. The second building block, functional integration, addresses the need to integrate the business and IT strategy. These building blocks can be identified for both business and IT, resulting in the strategic alignment model.

Looking at each quadrant of the strategic alignment model, one can identify three aspects per quadrant that need to be addressed when aligning business and IT. For the external business domain, an organisation needs to determine what its Customers, products and/or services are, the business scope, how it distinguishes itself from its competitors, the distinctive competencies, what strategies will be used to deliver the products and services to the Customers, and the governance. For the internal business domain, the organisation should consider operations infrastructure, processes, and skills. The operations infrastructure comprises the facilities that support the people in carrying out the business processes. Skills in this domain are the skills of the staff members who need to carry out the business processes and work with the operations infrastructure.

On the IT side a similar argument can be used. In the external IT domain the technology scope addresses the available technology that can be used to support the business. Systemic competencies mean the specific attributes IT needs to have to support the business strategy. Systemic competencies in the model can be compared with universal Service Level Requirements (SLRs) for the IT as a whole, such as cost, time to market, and availability. IT governance is similar to the governance in the external domain, except that it applies to strategies for creating and providing the IT services. The internal IT domain is, again, similar to the internal business domain. The aspects of IT Infrastructure, IT processes and skills are similar to the operations infrastructure, business processes and skills, except that they apply to the IT domain instead of the business domain. A broader discussion of this topic can be found in the strategic alignment model article by Henderson and Venkatraman.

All 12 aspects are linked to each other. Changes in one of the aspects influence the other aspects. The way the aspects are influenced depends on the perspective taken in the business–IT alignment. The perspective chosen depends on the strategic position of IT in the company and the business use and business function that need to be supported by IT.

### IT as a cost centre

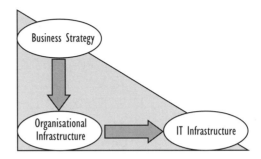

The traditional perspective on IT is to use the business strategy as the driver and business operations as the pivot for aligning business and IT. From this perspective, business management is considered to define the business strategy and IT is implementing this strategy by designing and implementing the required IT Infrastructure to support the chosen business strategy. In this situation, IT is performing as a cost centre. In a cost centre, all activities are geared toward reducing the Total Cost of Ownership (TCO) for IT. This means that applications are designed to be easy to maintain, to support automated operations, and are based on proven technology.

### IT as a profit centre

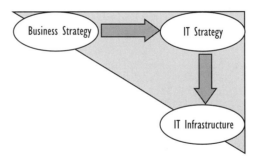

Another way to align business and IT is by changing the roles of business management and IT management when defining the business strategy. Instead of implementing an IT Infrastructure to support the chosen business strategy, one would first define an IT strategy to determine what technology should be employed to optimally enable the chosen business strategy. In this situation, IT is fulfilling the role of profit centre. In a profit centre all activities are focused on gaining as much revenue from the technology employed as possible, at an acceptable cost. This would result in applications designed to be highly flexible in order to adjust to changing business requirements. Applications would also be readily available and high performing. Where IT is considered to be a profit centre, proven technology would be used to ensure reliable solutions supporting the chosen business strategy as much as possible.

### IT as an investment centre

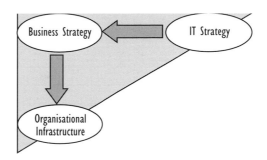

Instead of using the business strategy as the driving force, a company can also take the IT strategy as a starting point. This path takes the IT strategy as a driver, and the business strategy as the pivot to explore emerging technologies that impact on the products and services that will be put on the market, and the advantage the company will gain over its competitors. The business strategy and business organisation would be defined based on the new technologies that can be employed. In this situation, IT is regarded as an investment centre. Typically, applications would be developed for early time to market and use innovative ways to support business operations. This perspective is characterised by a focus on adopting new technologies rather than considering systems management issues.

### IT as a service centre

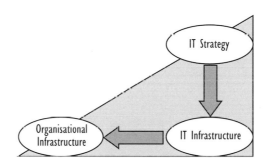

The last path that can be chosen is to use the IT strategy to build a world class IT services organisation. This perspective can be considered when IT is a corporate resource and no single business strategy can be identified. Here, IT determines an IT strategy aimed at providing optimal services to the business Users in the corporation. Focus, in this perspective, is directed toward shared IT services throughout the corporation, and the IT Infrastructure, processes, and skills are all designed for delivering reliable, available, and cost-effective IT services.

In conclusion, it should be noted that Henderson and Venkatraman recommend that no single perspective should be chosen for all of IT. Virtually every IT organisation has departments, groups, partners, or entire divisions operating from each of these perspectives simultaneously. In some cases, a single group may perform across more than one of these perspectives and thus should apply this model to the functions within their domain. The perspective chosen in any given instance will depend on the business function supported and the market position of the company with regard to that business function. In other words, the business and IT must jointly assess and agree on how to position the business functions identified within the organisation, as discussed in Paragraph 3.1.1. Once this is done, the context is set for both groups on how to move forward and directly align the business and IT objectives, which will subsequently be included in both the business and IT strategies.

### 3.1.3  Business–IT alignment and Service Management

The previous sections discussed three major items:

1  the need for aligning business and IT objectives

2  the use of an architecture to capture key business functions

3  a model, based on the strategic value of IT, to determine which of four main perspectives should be utilised in the alignment of business and IT strategies.

This section builds on these concepts, and adds the relationship of IT services and IT systems to the business functions. Since the majority of business functionality is deployed through applications, and applications make up IT systems and services, this is a critical linkage to understand. In addition, this section introduces the concept of identifying key business drivers within the business functions that in turn are supported by service and operational level requirements. Given the complexity of the inter-relationships between all these elements, the only practical way to present them is with the use of an entity diagram. The Strategic Alignment Objectives Model (SAOM) shown in Figure 3.3 depicts all of these elements in the context of aligning business and IT. Please note that it is not within the scope of this book to provide detailed guidance on, or descriptions of, all the entities in the diagram. The Service Level Management module of the ITIL *Service Delivery* book provides more information on the relationship between business functions and IT services.

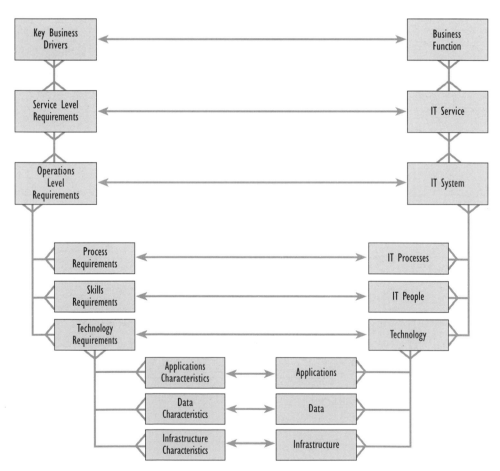

*Figure 3.3 – The Strategic Alignment Objectives Model (SAOM)*

The SAOM depicts the business functions directly supported by one or more IT services, which are made up of one or more IT systems. The business requirements for an IT service are provided by the analysis of the business function. These in turn are reflected as requirements of the IT systems. The IT systems themselves consist of processes, people, and technologies. The technology entity completes the IT systems side of the diagram, with applications, data and infrastructure.

Starting again with the business function entity, the identification of key business drivers should occur as part of the function analysis and definition. Key business drivers are the attributes of a business function that drive the behaviour and implementation of that business function in order to achieve the strategic business objectives of the company. In other words, key business drivers are the primary reasons the business wants to employ the business function through an IT service or services. In many ways, the key business drivers formulate the guiding principles or mission statement for the effort to deliver the systems and services, and they anchor the projects and work efforts to the clearly defined business objectives.

Furthermore, the key business drivers are incorporated in two key areas. The first incorporation is through the analysis of the business function, which results in functional requirements deployed through IT systems (applications, data, and infrastructure). The second is that key business drivers must be reflected within the IT Service Management activities and documentation. As the SAOM indicates, the primary method for this is through SLRs and supporting operational level requirements. These requirements are contained in Service Level Agreements (SLAs) and Operational Level Agreements (OLAs) respectively. SLRs are items that detail characteristics that must be achieved at the IT Service Level, such as availability and transaction response time. Operational level requirements are items that detail characteristics that must be achieved at the IT system level, such as network throughput and component availability. The ITIL *Service Delivery* book has a full explanation of Service Level Management (SLM) and contains detailed descriptions of both SLAs and OLAs.

Continuing the SAOM description, operational level requirements should reflect critical process, skills, and technology requirements derived along with the IT system entities. It should be emphasised that this does not imply all system requirements, but rather those that are critical for inclusion in an OLA.

Finally, in order to complete the business and IT alignment it is necessary to capture certain characteristics about the applications, data, and infrastructure that make up the IT systems. These again are selected characteristics that should be found within the context of the key business drivers, service and operational level requirements, and system requirements.

In summary, the key message of the SAOM is that business objectives can, and should, be reflected at all levels of IT. This includes the highest level of an IT service all the way through the lowest levels of applications, data, and infrastructure. This will help ensure that the key business drivers, and thus the business objectives, are reflected at all levels within the organisation, the IT systems, and the people within both the business and IT arenas.

## 3.2    Key business drivers

### 3.2.1    Defining key business drivers

Key business drivers can be defined as …

> **'… the attributes of a business function that drive the behaviour and implementation of that business function in order to achieve the strategic business objectives of the company…'**

It is important to note that this definition is not intended to be a definitive standard or even a universally accepted definition. It is, for the purposes of this book, a working definition of the critical business objectives for a given business function. It is an indicator that allows both the business and IT groups to have a common set of objectives that are tangible and used throughout a project, or set of projects, as guiding principles for the organisation. Key business drivers shape the vision of the company and thus the mission and scope of the IT projects within the organisation. Regardless of the acceptance of this definition, however, best practice would suggest that key goals and objectives must be clearly defined, concise, and, most importantly, written down and communicated.

Regardless of the term and definition selected by a specific organisation, key business drivers must adhere to certain attributes to be of any practical use. The following table provides five key attributes that should be used to determine if a key business driver has been adequately captured and appropriately defined:

**S**    Specific
**M**    Measurable
**A**    Agreed to
**R**    Realistic
**T**    Time specific

The SMART attributes should be applied to key business drivers, as well as other goals, objectives, and requirements. These would include, but not be limited to, functional requirements, Service Level Requirements (SLRs), operational level requirements, and technology requirements. To stress the need for SMART key business drivers, consider the example of a commonly stated, yet often ill-defined, business driver – cost-effectiveness. There is rarely an IT service or system that does not list cost-effectiveness as a key objective. However, to simply state that a system needs to be cost-effective leads at best to an ambiguous requirement and at worst a vague and immeasurable requirement that is open to debate. In fact, many projects have failed because organisations inadequately defined cost-effectiveness.

For example, does being cost-effective mean building the service or solution in a cost-effective manner? Or does it mean implementing the business function in a manner that results in internal operational cost savings? Could it mean producing a product with higher quality attributes without increasing costs? Does it mean all of these? And if it does, over what time period should the savings occur? These simple questions show the need for SMART business drivers and SLRs all the way through to low level infrastructure and data requirements. Without them, the IT service or system might be deployed with no way to determine cost-effectiveness of any kind.

The following shows a SMART business driver that targets one area of cost-effectiveness in a hypothetical manufacturing process:

**S**   Reduce the cost of goods sold for our Galaxy V product by 10% at the Birmingham plant.

**M**   The cost of goods baseline cost number will be the last three months COGS financial reports from the Galaxy V production line. This includes production time, raw materials, and sub-assembly. The cost reduction must be attained for three consecutive months.

**A**   The plant manager, IT director, Galaxy V production manager, facilities manager, and the plant finance officer approve this key business driver.

**R**   The initial feasibility report forecasts total potential cost savings of 7% to 21% directly from COGS assuming both the automation levels and lower supply costs of raw materials are achieved.

**T**   Achieve the proven cost reduction within the next 18 calendar months.

The above SMART key business driver should ultimately result in many SMART requirements that would be placed upon the IT service or system under consideration. This business driver will in turn likely be decomposed into hundreds of SMART requirements that make up the project, or projects, that will ultimately be necessary to accomplish the key business driver. This will probably include IT system requirements from screen response times to enterprise resource planning (ERP) logic changes. It is very important that, as these requirements are derived, they are consistently measured in their contribution to meeting the key business driver.

### 3.2.2   Demonstrating the use of key business drivers

The use of key business drivers to align business and IT can best be demonstrated by an example. The business manager of a bank's worldwide operating dealing rooms identifies, among others, accessibility to trading information as a key business driver. The specification of accessibility is that the business manager wants the information on stock trades to be fully available during trading hours in the designated region. On the other hand, the manager wants the trading information details of regions in earlier time zones to be accessible to the regions in later zones. In order to make sure that IT contributes to the strategic business goals, IT should support the key business drivers of the dealing room. The indicators of the IT services provided to the dealing room should therefore support the key business driver of accessibility. IT services are specified by their SLRs, which mandate that some of these SLRs must adhere to the key business driver of accessibility.

Assume that each of the dealing rooms in the bank receives the same service from the global IT Service Provider. This means that the IT Service Provider and the dealing room manager can agree upon one SLA for the IT service that delivers, among others, stock trade information. This SLA could cover the functions that will be made available to the stock trader, the availability of these functionalities and the information on stock trades, as SLRs. However, most IT services defined on a business level are made up of multiple IT systems. The fact that an IT service can be made up of more than one IT system means that the service level manager needs to define Operational Level Agreements (OLAs) between the IT systems. In most cases the IT systems are the departments managing the applications, databases, and infrastructure supporting the IT service to the dealing room. The operations level requirements specified in the OLA, supporting the SLR and thus the key business driver accessibility, can be described in terms of availability and interoperability. Availability will be specified in terms of percentage of time the IT systems will be available and the number of planned and unplanned outages that are acceptable. Interoperability will be specified in terms of ability to exchange information between each IT system and the availability of interfaces between them.

In order to make the OLAs work, processes, people, and technology have to be aligned with the requirements specified in the OLA. Indicators can be specified for the processes, people, and technology in order to meet the OLAs. These indicators then can be used throughout the whole lifecycle. Indicators such as process goals or requirements, skills requirements, and technology requirements, can be used to align the IT systems with the key business indicators of the business manager's dealing room. In order to manage the applications as part of the IT service provided to the business, IT can use the technology requirements next to the functional requirements to measure the added value to the business. The same applies for the lifecycle itself and the people necessary to fulfil roles in that lifecycle. By the use of the presented breakdown, IT organisations can be fully aligned with the business on a tactical and operational level, and their contribution to the business can be measured in an agreed-upon way.

This example shows that each party involved in the lifecycle can have a scorecard of objectives to contribute to the business operations. For the business, the strategic goals will be translated into key business drivers. The key business drivers will determine the SLRs that will specify what business value is expected from the IT service. The SLA, in which the SLRs are specified, will determine the scorecard for the IT Service Provider, while the OLAs will do the same for the IT systems that make up the IT service. Process managers can use the process goals or process requirements as their scorecard to manage their processes in the lifecycle, while human resources managers can use the skills requirements to manage the human capital of the IT Service Provider. During the application lifecycle, the requirement, functional and non-functional, specified in the requirements phase, will be used as a scorecard to measure the business value of that application. This will also mean that this scorecard can be used in decisions to optimise or decommission an application.

### 3.2.3    Using key business drivers

Implementing the use of key business drivers requires careful consideration by the leadership team of the organisation. The key business drivers will mobilise project team(s) in a way that might result in any or all of new systems projects, major upgrades to existing systems and retirement of legacy systems. In addition, there will likely be projects that have little or no IT component that will occur in concert with the IT systems projects. This, of course, all depends on the reach and extent of the key business drivers, but often seemingly simple key business drivers can result in significant cross-functional projects.

It is beyond the scope of this book to fully explore all the aspects of using key business drivers. The subject warrants a book of its own. However, it is worth noting a few points that should be considered when implementing key business drivers in a business or organisation. All these points take an enterprise-wide view of the key business drivers an organisation is attempting to use, or act upon:

- organisational capabilities
- organisational capacity
- dependent business drivers
- conflicting business drivers.

#### Organisational capabilities

When an organisation implements key business drivers, a fundamental question is whether it has the required capabilities. Do internal staff have the required skills and competencies? What about its partners and suppliers? Even more specifically, does the organisation have the technical capabilities, as well as the required overall maturity of its business operations and processes? Finally, does the organisation have sufficient geographical and market reach to deliver these capabilities? That is a key consideration. See the readiness assessment in Chapter 4 for more detail.

## Organisational capacity

Another enterprise-wide consideration is the organisation's capacity. The key question is how many key business drivers can the entire organisation handle at any given time? The answer requires specific information about a given organisation, and therefore it is impossible to answer completely here. However, a few common mistakes to avoid are:

- Unbalanced workloads: Looking across all key business drivers, the work must be balanced to avoid creating a bottleneck in a particular group, which in turn might impact several projects simultaneously.

- Unique knowledge or resource(s): Avoid simultaneous deployment of key business drivers where a unique resource or set of resources possessing scarce knowledge or capabilities, are needed at the same time.

- Indecision and no decision: Capacity issues are often the result of the leadership team's reluctance to make tough decisions about a key business driver priority. Such decisions often entail postponing certain projects and cancelling other projects outright. These are difficult decisions in the light of market pressures and business demand, but avoiding them puts every project in the organisation at risk of delay, cost overruns, or outright failure.

## Dependent business drivers

Key business drivers that are mutually dependent require careful consideration and planning to implement properly. These dependencies exaggerate and compound the issues of capabilities and capacity. In these cases, it is often beneficial to consolidate the key business drivers or decompose them further so that they can be decoupled.

## Conflicting business drivers

This condition occurs when two or more key business drivers actually oppose each other in their objectives. Although it would seem obvious and simple to avoid this condition, it is a very common occurrence, particularly in larger organisations. In this situation, it is likely that the key business drivers are not adequately defined or must be redefined so that they become realistic for the organisation to deliver against.

These four considerations need to be viewed across the entire enterprise or organisation. Such a macro-level view allows the leadership team to prioritise the business drivers, taking into consideration the aggregate capabilities, capacity, and interdependencies that exist within the organisation. This in turn allows the organisation to select the high-priority business drivers and focus resources on them appropriately, which ensures that a realistic and achievable set of business goals and objectives are set for the organisation as a whole.

In order to effectively accomplish this macro-level prioritisation of key business drivers, the organisation needs to analyse and assess information about its abilities, the IT services and systems, cost structures and people. In many cases, sufficient information is not available to enable the organisation to make sound decisions in this area. An application portfolio will provide organisations with a significant proportion of the information they need about their applications, systems and services in order to make these kinds of decisions.

## 3.3 Managing the application portfolio

### 3.3.1 Introducing the application portfolio

Section 3.1 described the approaches for aligning business need with IT expenditures in order to achieve maximum business value from the IT investment. This alignment is critical for ensuring that appropriate investment levels are made across the company based on identified and well-defined business drivers. However, a key question remains – once this alignment is completed, how does an organisation effectively manage the vast array of applications and services? It is obvious that the business value provided by a given service will not remain static and will require attention on an ongoing basis. Given the complexity of integrated applications and services, the ability to effectively manage this dynamic environment is a huge challenge for the IT Service Provider.

A highly successful method for managing a complex applications environment is through the use of an application portfolio. The application portfolio provides a mechanism for viewing and evaluating the entire suite of applications in the business enterprise. If properly constructed and managed, the application portfolio is extremely effective in managing the IT investment, at the application and services level, across all business areas supported. By this, the application portfolio becomes a tool for managing a suite of applications in alignment with dynamic business needs.

So what exactly is an application portfolio? Simply stated, it is an information system that contains key attributes about applications being utilised within the company. This includes insourced, outsourced, business, and infrastructure applications. Any application that is necessary in the daily operations of the enterprise, or deemed mission-critical, should be evaluated for inclusion in the application portfolio. In other words, if the application is considered a corporate asset, it should be included in the portfolio. This is critical for ensuring that maximum benefit is realised from the portfolio and that business decisions and priorities are based upon accurate IT information. It should also be mentioned that the application portfolio is considered to provide a single virtual source for application information. In practice, the portfolio could be implemented through several distinct, but integrated portfolio systems. Sometimes these distinct portfolios will be aligned to major business functional areas like sales and marketing, finance, human resources, etc.

To further understand how an application portfolio is used, consider another type of portfolio that has been in use for many years, specifically, the investment portfolio. There are many similarities between both types of portfolios, since they are based upon the same fundamental principle of managing a diverse set of individual assets holistically to maximise the total Return On Investment within the stated objectives of the portfolio.

A final note: no successful business would consider managing its financial assets without utilising an investment portfolio. Any business would be wise to follow the same rule with its application assets.

### 3.3.2    The application portfolio in practice

This section attempts to illustrate how an application portfolio can be utilised to address common information needs that are often difficult, if not impossible, for many IT Service Providers to determine accurately. This information is required for making informed management decisions, but is all too often omitted from the decision-making process, or is inaccurate when it is provided.

However, before dealing with this exercise, it is useful to explore further the types of attributes that are typically applied to the applications in the portfolio. This will provide a more intuitive understanding of the power an application portfolio can deliver. This section is not intended to cover all aspects of data modelling, with attribute and domain value definitions, but rather offer a layperson's list of key attributes found in the typical application portfolio. Table 3.1 depicts these common attributes.

*Table 3.1 – Common application attributes*

**Common application attributes**

| Application name | IT operations owner | New development cost |
|---|---|---|
| Application identifier | IT development owner | Annual Operational Costs |
| Application description | Support contacts | Annual support cost |
| Business functions performed | Database technologies | Annual maintenance costs |
| IT services supported | Dependent applications | Outsourced functions |
| Executive sponsor | Systems architecture | Outsource partners |
| Geographies supported | User interfaces | Production metrics |
| Business criticality | Network topology | OLA hyperlink |
| SLA hyperlink | Application technologies | Support metrics |
| Business owner | | |

Table 3.1 provides a mere glimpse into the types of data elements to consider, and some level of customisation is required for every given instance. As with any information system, due diligence should be applied when constructing the data elements to be maintained, and domain values should be carefully considered.

Assuming that careful consideration was given to constructing an organisation's application portfolio, which makes available a wealth of information, what can be done with it? What types of questions can be answered? Will this enable the organisation to make better, more informed, business decisions? Consider the types of tangible questions that can now be addressed.

To accomplish this, consider a few common areas of interest for the IT and business decision-makers with regard to applications. The following examples pose two simple, and often-asked, questions of IT Service Providers that are rarely answered accurately or in a timely fashion. These clearly illustrate the type of analysis possible with the implementation of an application portfolio. The format for these examples begins with a hypothetical question posed by a business and/or IT decision-maker. A series of implied sub-questions is listed in the next section, which can be answered with simple queries from a properly constructed application portfolio. The last section of each example provides a list of potential business benefits, which could be achieved by acting properly upon the information provided.

**Example 1**

*Decision-maker question*

Why are we spending so much on our sales and marketing systems?

*Implied queries*

- Which applications support sales and marketing?
- What business services do these applications provide or support?
- What are the development, infrastructure, and support costs for each?
- What percentage of IT costs is associated with sales and marketing initiatives?
- Which applications are considered mission critical, business critical, or nice-to-haves?
- Which applications were developed in-house and which are third-party provided?
- Which applications store core Customer data?
- Which applications have read, write, and/or update access?
- Which User groups use these applications?
- Where are these applications hosted?

*Potential business benefits*

By acting upon the information provided, the following business benefits are possible:

- Operational cost savings
  - Consolidate redundant IT services
  - Eliminate redundant systems or functions performed
  - Consolidate business functions
  - Examine potential outsourcing arrangements
- Business and IT realignment
  - Revisit key business drivers – are they still correct?
  - Revisit importance of IT supported sales and marketing initiatives
  - Realign IT expenditures with the key business drivers
  - Cancel or delay non-essential IT projects

**Example 2**

*Decision-maker question*

Why does it take so long to add a few simple attributes about our products?

*Implied queries*

- What applications contain product information?
- What business functions do these applications support?
- Which applications require modification to support the additional attributes?
- Which applications have read, write, and/or update access?
- How many different technologies are utilised by these applications?
- Are these applications in-house or outsourced?
- What User groups are involved?
- Who owns development and support for the applications?

*Potential business benefits*

By acting upon the information provided, the following business benefits are possible:

- Reduced time to market for system changes
    - Consolidate redundant IT services
    - Eliminate unnecessary functions
    - Consolidate business functions
    - Implement a data management and replication strategy for product data
- Business and IT realignment
    - Revisit key business drivers – are they still correct?
    - Revisit importance of IT supported sales and marketing initiatives
    - Realign IT expenditures with the key business drivers
    - Cancel or delay non-essential IT projects

In the two examples given, the information provided by the application portfolio allows the enterprise to analyse two key areas. The first is the area of questions originally asked by the decision-maker. In the examples, these were questions about Operational Costs and time to market for requested system changes. Both of these questions are targeted at the broader category of efficiency in the IT group, an area that must be examined on a continual basis by the IT Service Provider. The key benefit of the application portfolio comes in the timely, concise and accurate answers to these legitimate business questions. This provides the basis for opportunistic action plans to improve the delivery of IT services.

The second, and more compelling, area of questions that these examples highlights is the area of business and IT alignment. The questions directly address both the business initiatives supported by IT and the investment levels associated with each. Generally speaking, the type of questions posed by the hypothetical decision-maker is an indication that the business–IT alignment needs to be revisited and possibly adjusted. The key benefit of the application portfolio is that it enables this to happen. It allows the business and IT to jointly assess performance against the business drivers and make strategic and tactical corrections to both the business drivers and the IT strategies to deliver them. Because the information needed to make sound business decisions is now part of the daily operations of the business and IT, these course corrections can be identified and acted upon virtually on demand. Enabling the business and IT to be more responsive to changing market and business conditions gives a definite competitive advantage.

### 3.3.3 Implementation considerations

There are a few key items that should be considered before implementing an application portfolio. The following paragraphs provide general guidance in areas that are critical for the successful development and operation of an application portfolio.

#### Dealing with cultural resistance

As with any strategic and enterprise-wide project, cultural resistance must be acknowledged and addressed in order for the project to be successful. The same will hold true for implementing an application portfolio. Understanding an organisation's unique cultural attributes is extremely important in determining implementation strategies that will lower the cultural resistance to Change. Strong executive sponsorship, senior management tenacity, and employee involvement are all important elements of a successful project.

#### Making portfolio management business critical

Many companies spend the time and resources to determine their key business drivers and align their IT expenditures accordingly. However, this is often a painful and expensive project performed at irregular intervals, usually in response to escalating IT costs or poor business performance. There is value in this approach, but it falls far short of the potential that exists when proper management discipline is applied to maintaining and updating this alignment as required. As the historical separation between business and IT disappears, it is becoming increasingly important to actively manage the business–IT alignment on a much more frequent basis. The application portfolio is an excellent tool that enables companies to accomplish this and fully realise the benefits of their IT investments.

#### Technical considerations

As stated above, application portfolio management is an information system and as such requires the same level of application development discipline and IT Service Management support as any other business- or mission-critical system. That said, the following are a few suggestions worth repeating here for anyone planning the technical aspects of an application portfolio management system:

- Select the application attributes, data elements and domain values carefully, and consider business, development, technical, support and operational requirements.
- Plan application interfaces carefully. Remain true to company data management policies around read/write/update access. Determine which data requires real-time versus batch interfaces.
- Utilise existing data stores as much as possible. Systems that will likely be in existence and should be considered carefully include:

- Configuration Management Database (CMDB)
- Financial accounting systems
- Human resource systems
- Product support systems
- Change Management and Control systems

■ Consider the scale requirements for the system and build accordingly. Do not feel compelled to build a full-scale management information system when a simple spreadsheet would suffice.

■ Consider integrating the application portfolio into existing management information systems, digital dashboards, workbench tools, intranet systems, etc.

# 4 ALIGNING THE DELIVERY STRATEGY WITH KEY BUSINESS DRIVERS AND ORGANISATIONAL CAPABILITIES

Strategy means more than defining and designing a vision, and determining whether a new situation calls for a business or IT strategy. Strategy also means making sure that the organisation has the ability to realise strategic directions set out by senior executives. The chapter starts with a readiness assessment that can be used to verify whether an organisation is capable of building and operating a new IT system. It concludes with the steps for defining the delivery strategy and preparing to deliver the application.

## 4.1 Readiness assessment

**'A man has got to know his limitations.' (Clint Eastwood)**

### 4.1.1 Providing a baseline for Risk Management

Many software development projects are destined for failure before they ever begin. The way to avoid that is for each organisation to ask whether it is capable of handling the challenge at hand. That means asking such questions as: Is our company capable of building the software for the Space Shuttle? Do we need to be? Are we able to effectively use the applications we develop? What are the capabilities of our business and IT organisation? What capabilities do we need to build and operate these applications? Are the IT services aligned with our key business drivers? If they are, to what extent are they aligned?

Many organisations are over-optimistic when deciding to build new applications. In a number of cases, the task at hand can be too complex given the maturity level of both the business and the IT organisation. Often, alternatives to fulfil business needs are not even considered. Each organisation should, however, assess its ability to build, maintain, and operate the IT services needed to support the business, and assess whether the business is able to make effective use of each application in order to make the most out of its IT investments.

> **Example**
>
> Many implementations of enterprise resource planning (ERP) packages, with hindsight, did not live up to the promised value. The full integration possibilities of business processes and the integrated management of the business were hardly ever established. Why? Most organisations implemented modules of the packages based on the 'as is' situation of the business operations, instead of changing the business operations to align them with the (standard) operational model of the ERP packages.
>
> Even when the business operations were aligned with the packages, the implementation of the new software often failed anyway. Why? In many cases, the cause was cultural resistance by the workforce. Why would the workforce resist? The business organisation was not able to absorb that much change at once and the ERP packages assumed a higher level of maturity in the organisation than existed.

The way for organisations to avoid taking a false step even before a project starts, is to conduct a readiness assessment to determine the risks. A readiness assessment verifies the alignment of business requirements (key business drivers) and the ability of the IT organisation to build and deliver the IT services that support the business. Ideally, an organisation should strive for full business and IT alignment. In reality, however, there will always be a gap, whether small or big. Depending on the quality of the match, a delivery strategy for employing the application(s) should be defined. The actual delivery strategy for an application, therefore, is chosen based on the alignment of business and IT and on the ability of the organisation to deliver (see also ITIL *Planning to Implement Service Management*).

> ### Example
>
> The marketing manager of a publishing company visited a conference to assess the latest digital publishing technology. He was impressed by the variety of systems and their flexibility. The extensive use of XML promised a number of great advantages for the company's clients. The marketing manager knew what he needed and formulated the requirements for a new system that had to be based on XML. The IT department had no experience with XML, or tools available to allow them to work with XML efficiently. However, the IT department had a reputation to live up to and promised the delivery of the new system. During development of the system, the IT department's lack of knowledge and its immaturity at gathering new knowledge led to a delayed system delivery and the spoiling of a carefully built reputation.

The readiness assessment has to deal with the risks generated by a mismatch of business requirements and capabilities of the IT organisation, and assess the ability of the business organisation to work effectively with the new applications in fulfilling the business requirements. The issue of organisational readiness is covered in more detail in the ITIL book *The Business Perspective*.

Focusing on the IT organisation and matching business requirements (demand) with capabilities is a continual process, and there will always be a gap between new business requirements and existing IT capabilities. Over time, business requirements will change and the IT delivery capability will need to keep pace. As discussed in Chapter 3, the business requirements can be expressed as key business drivers. The IT capabilities should be reflected in SLRs. The breakdown of SLRs shows that, in order to meet those SLRs, both IT Services and the technology need to meet organisational and technology requirements. On top of that, in order to build the applications chosen for a given IT service, application development needs to meet some organisational requirements. The organisational requirements of both application development and IT services can be expressed in maturity levels. The more mature an organisation, the more complex the IT services it can create and deliver.

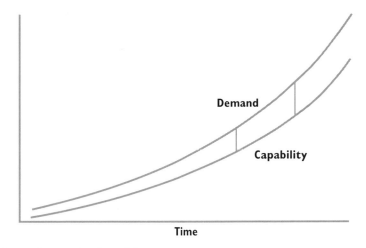

*Figure 4.1 – Evolution of demand and capability over time*

Discussions about meeting new business requirements are too often dominated by an emphasis on the things that change rather than on the things that remain stable. Change, however, is a fact of life and no one can reliably predict the future. Does this also mean that an IT organisation, both application development and IT services, cannot predict changes in demand? And does this also mean that an IT organisation cannot manage the changes in demand? Not really. In fact, using the application portfolio and key business drivers enables both business and IT to create and foster a close relationship, and determine future directions in IT based on changing business demands. This will give the IT organisation a chance to assess future directions in changing business requirements, together with a chance to influence the way changes in business requirements can be supported by changing IT capabilities.

Each organisation has its own capacity for handling Change. It is important for organisations to be able to measure that capacity, because the ability to handle Change effectively can be the difference between a successful project and a failed one. One way an organisation can determine that capacity is to ask a series of questions, such as: How well does the organisation handle the introduction of new software development tools? How does it handle the introduction of new technology? How does it handle requests for new applications? How does it plan the delivery of software in a continually changing environment? How does it handle a shortage of software development skills?

In addition to an IT organisation's ability to handle Change originating from a changing environment, it is also required to manage changes without disturbing the delivery of day-to-day IT services. That raises questions regarding how well the organisation handles User complaints. How does it handle shortage of network capacity? How does it handle suppliers? How does it train IT staff and Users? How does it handle Requests for Change?

If an organisation can effectively answer questions about its maturity, it then knows the risks associated with the delivery of software. Once it knows the risks, it can define a delivery strategy for dealing with those risks. Does the software development need to be outsourced? How can successful delivery of the software be measured in terms of the business value that it needs to provide? This should lead to the creation of contingency plans to contain the potential damage.

That might seem to raise the question of whether Risk Management should be part of project management. The answer is, of course, yes, in the sense that Risk Management should always be part of good project management. But the larger questions of Risk have to be addressed at a level higher than project management, because a project has a limited scope. A project manager only has control over the project itself, but the deployment of new technology by a project team can have consequences that exceed those boundaries. Those consequences can have an impact on both the business and the IT organisation itself. Beyond that, in many cases the biggest risks of a project are not those risks related to technology, but those related to organisational Change. Those risks should be addressed by the business and IT organisation, and not just at the individual project level. See OGC's *Management of Risk: Guidance for Practitioners* for further relevant information.

NB: It is important to be aware of the significance of the readiness of the overall organisation (and not only of the IT organisation) to allow successful implementation of IT services.

### 4.1.2    Providing a baseline for improving the IT capability

The readiness assessment not only verifies whether the organisation is able to deploy new or changed applications, it also provides the starting point for improvement of the capabilities of both the business and IT organisation. Improving the IT capabilities, in fact, means improving the maturity level of the IT organisation. In order to be able to assess and improve its maturity, an organisation needs to define maturity in an unambiguous, verifiable, and traceable manner.

When considering its maturity, one way to describe an IT organisation is as a set of processes that can be measured and improved. Regarding software development, Watts S. Humphrey of the Software Engineering Institute said:

> '**An important first step in addressing software problems is to treat the entire software task as a process that can be controlled, measured, and improved. Clearly, a fully effective process must consider the relationships of all the required tasks, the tools and methods used, and the skill, training, and motivation of the people involved.**'

However, focusing on process maturity alone is a somewhat one-dimensional approach to determining an IT organisation's ability to build, operate, and maintain applications. In order to provide the full context of IT capabilities, a readiness assessment should examine six elements that help to characterise an IT organisation: methodology, technology, skills, organisation, measurement, and culture.

#### Methodology

A method describes the specific procedures an organisation uses to build and deliver a piece of software. Among other things, a method describes the way User requirements are modelled, how the external and internal system designs are modelled, and how all the different models fit together.

#### Technology, skills, and organisation

Technology, skills, and organisation are the ingredients an organisation needs in order to follow a method and deliver a piecc of software.

Technology includes the use of tools, network protocols, hardware platforms, and architectural principles. Most organisations have defined standards for technology, for example in the form of standard architectures for applications and infrastructures.

Skills are the abilities employees bring to the delivery of IT services. This category covers procedures to develop skills by measurement and training.

Organisation describes the roles and responsibilities required to deliver IT services, as well as the formal and informal structures they make up. It also defines how resources are requested and allocated.

### Measurement

Measurements cover client satisfaction, Quality of Services, quality of products, and other quantities that help to establish the status quo, set baselines, guide improvements and measure the impact of changes in the IT services capability.

### Culture

Culture addresses an organisation's commitment to perform. Cultural aspects include an organisation's values, its objectives, and its communication style. If an IT organisation's culture is not in line with the needs of the business, both client satisfaction and employee morale will probably be low.

## 4.1.3    Assessing IT capabilities

Before starting a development project, an organisation should be able to assess accurately the maturity of its development and delivery processes. If the organisation is not able to do that, it should perform a readiness assessment. This does not mean that an organisation must be able to implement all necessary processes in house, however. If an organisation decides to outsource part of its IT capability, it can assume the presence and maturity of those particular processes as part of its overall maturity level. But it is crucial that the outsourcing organisation ensures that the external organisations handling those activities have indeed implemented the processes expected, and that those processes have the appropriate maturity level to support the solution that meets the needs of the key business drivers.

Many organisations, both commercial- and research-oriented, have developed maturity models based on process maturity. Each of these models classifies maturity into several discrete levels, each level being defined and described. Most maturity models place an emphasis on process maturity. The Software Engineering Institute (SEI), for instance, provides certificates that declare that a particular organisation's capability has a particular maturity level. However, SEI's Capability Maturity Model generally focuses on the application development organisation, while in the ITIL book *Planning to Implement Service Management* references can be found to maturity models of the IT services organisation. The value of this declaration is maintained through standard training programmes and certification for all professionals who are authorised to assess and declare the maturity level in line with the SEI's Capability Maturity Model. An example of the maturity levels is given in Table 4.1.

*Table 4.1 – Maturity levels and their characteristics*

| Level | Characteristic | Problem area |
|---|---|---|
| 1. Initial | Ad hoc/chaotic | Project planning/management |
| 2. Repeatable | Depends on individuals | Standards, training, testing |
| 3. Defined | Institutionalised | Process measurement and analysis |
| 4. Managed | Measured process | Technology changes |
| 5. Optimising | Process improvement | Automation |

In Table 4.1, each maturity level is characterised by a description of the maturity of the processes in the organisation. The ad hoc/chaotic nature of processes for level 1 means that it is actually difficult to recognise any process at all. In such organisations, similar activities are carried out in different ways and lessons are not learned. The wheel is reinvented each time and the same mistakes are made over and over again. The problem areas that require attention are project planning and project management. The appropriate focus will help the organisation to progress to the next maturity level.

An organisation at the second level is able to execute projects successfully, with satisfying results. The problem, however, is that success heavily depends on the skills of a small number of key individuals. Standardising and documenting the preferred way of working, and training the employees to work accordingly, could help such an organisation grow to the next maturity level.

The third level is a fairly mature level that not many organisations will reach. Many organisations get stuck at level 2, because they just cannot cope with the pace of changes that occur in the IT world. Some organisations try to standardise things that should not and cannot be standardised. Standardising a particular set of development techniques, a particular programming language, or the use of a particular development environment might temporarily progress an organisation to the third level, but the organisation will return to Level 2 as soon as those parameters change. However, if an organisation focuses on the ability to cope with change, and learns how to manage change instead of being ruled by it, it can reach and maintain itself at the third maturity level.

Reaching the third level offers the opportunity to start measuring the quality of the work performed. This will improve the predictability of the work planned and will lead to lower development costs and increased levels of Customer satisfaction. That is because measurements will lead to process optimisation and promises that can actually be delivered by the organisation.

Organisations at the fourth maturity level have IT organisations that know what is done and how well it is done. At the fifth level, organisations analyse measurements in a structured way and make improvements continually.

The question that remains is whether an organisation should assess its maturity each time an application is changed. Also, if a readiness assessment is carried out, is process maturity enough to focus on? Thorough assessments are expensive and have an impact on the whole IT organisation. The answer is that performing a readiness assessment thoroughly once or twice each year would suffice for understanding the maturity of the organisation each time an application is released for development. There are a number of self-assessments available for quickly reassessing the maturity level with limited costs. An organisation that opts to perform a thorough readiness assessment once a year can reassess along the way the impact of improvements by using these inexpensive self-assessments, justifying those investments.

A good maturity assessment should focus on several elements related to a process, as shown in

Figure 4.2. Some process maturity assessments focus on elements such as method, technology (or tools), skills, organisation and measurements, as well as some specific process characteristics such as process goals, process execution, and integration with other processes. The result of the assessment can be portrayed using a spider diagram showing the maturity of the process on each of these elements. An example of such a spider diagram is shown in Figure 4.2.

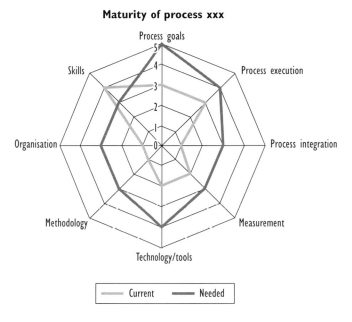

*Figure 4.2 – Result of a process maturity assessment*

Large development projects that introduce new technologies or ways of working should start with a change readiness assessment. A change readiness assessment determines the organisation's commitment, readiness, and ability to accept and sustain the changes that will be required by an initiative. The assessment could be based upon an initial look at the changes likely to occur with the project and their potential impact. The outcome of the assessment highlights issues that will impede change relative to:

- sponsorship of the change
- attitudes toward change formed by past experiences
- culture of the organisation.

Many assessment tools are available on the market. Most of these tools consist of questionnaires that classify the culture or the ability to change in different traits, elements, or aspects. Based on this classification, an organisation can identify strengths and weaknesses regarding the ability to change.

## 4.2 Defining the delivery strategy

### 4.2.1 Delivery strategy options

The readiness assessment provides a structured mechanism for determining an organisation's capabilities and state of readiness for delivering a new or revised application in support of the defined key business drivers. The information obtained from such an assessment can be used in determining the delivery strategy for a particular application, IT system, or IT service. The delivery strategy is the approach taken to move an organisation from a known state, based on the readiness assessment, to a desired state, determined by the business drivers. There are many ways to prepare an organisation for deploying a new application. The method and strategy selected should be based on the solution the organisation chooses for fulfilling its key business drivers, as well as the capabilities of the IT organisation and its partners. The scale of options available is quite large and not every option need be considered in every case. However, keeping all the options available for consideration is key for building and operating innovative solutions to the most difficult business challenges. In the end, this may be the difference between a failed project – or even a failed company – and a successful one.

Although the readiness assessment determines the gap between the current and necessary capabilities, an IT organisation should not necessarily try to bridge that gap by itself. As noted earlier, there are many different delivery strategies that can be used. Each one has its own set of advantages and disadvantages, but all require some level of adaptation and customisation for the situation at hand. Table 4.2 lists the main categories of delivery strategies with a short abstract for each. Delivery practices tend to fall into one of these categories or some variant of them.

*Table 4.2 – Main delivery strategies*

| Delivery strategy | Description |
| --- | --- |
| Insourcing | This approach relies on utilising internal resources in the delivery of a new application, revised application, or data centre operations. |
| Outsourcing | This approach utilises external resources in a formal arrangement to deliver a well-defined portion of an application's development, maintenance, operations, and/or support. This includes the consumption of services from Application Service Providers (ASPs). |
| Co-sourcing | A combination of insourcing and outsourcing. This generally will involve contracting with an external firm to deliver a portion of an application's development, maintenance, operations, and/or support while acting within the premises of the company. |
| Partnership | A formal arrangement between two or more companies to co-develop, maintain, operate, or support an application, IT service, or business function(s). The focus here tends to be on strategic partnerships that leverage critical expertise or market opportunities. |
| Merger & Acquisition | Generally speaking, this occurs when one company acquires another company for cash and/or equity swaps of the company's stock. Again, this occurs generally in response to industry consolidations, market expansion, or in direct response to competitive pressures. |

Table 4.2 highlights a key point: the set of delivery strategies varies widely and ranges from a relatively straightforward effort solely managed within the boundaries of a company all the way to full company acquisitions. This broad range of alternatives provides significant flexibility, but at the added cost of additional complexity and in some cases Risk.

**Example**

A medium large bank merged with another bank that had a complementary product portfolio. Therefore the integration of applications was simple. However, the two banks felt that consolidation of operations would be beneficial, but would not leverage the economies of scale to a sufficient extent. Outsourcing was also an option, but instead the two banks chose to partner with an outsourcing company. The banks provided the bank-specific knowledge to make their IT services organisation an attractive data centre for smaller banks. The outsourcing partner provided the necessary technology expertise and new clients to benefit from the economies of scale.

### 4.2.2    Choosing a delivery strategy

So how does an organisation determine the optimum delivery strategy? There is no single or simple answer to this question. It is far too dependent upon the unique and specific situation under consideration. For this reason, the most appropriate guidance that can be provided is to describe key advantages and disadvantages of each delivery strategy. This in turn can be used as a checklist to determine which delivery approach should be evaluated further and most benefit the specific project or business initiative. Table 4.3 lists each strategy and its key advantages and disadvantages for the delivery of an application or IT service.

*Table 4.3 – Advantages and disadvantages of delivery strategies*

| Delivery strategy | Advantages | Disadvantages |
|---|---|---|
| Insourcing | Direct control<br>Freedom of choice<br>Rapid prototyping of leading-edge services<br>Familiar policies and processes<br>Company-specific knowledge | Scale limitations<br>Cost and time to market for services readily available outside<br>Dependent on internal resources and their skills and competencies |
| Outsourcing | Economies of scale<br>Purchased expertise<br>Supports focus on company core competencies<br>Support for transient needs<br>Test drive/trial of new services | Less direct control<br>Exit barriers<br>Solvency risk of suppliers<br>Unknown supplier skills and competencies<br>More challenging business process integration |
| Co-sourcing | Time to market<br>Leveraged expertise<br>Control | Project complexity<br>Intellectual property and copyright protection |
| Partnership | Time to market<br>Market expansion/entrance<br>Competitive response<br>Leveraged expertise<br>Risk sharing | Project complexity<br>Intellectual property and copyright protection<br>Culture clash between companies<br>Organisational integration<br>Operational systems integration<br>Shirking |
| Merger & Acquisition | Competitive response<br>Market expansion and new services<br>Direct control | Financial resource requirements<br>Culture clash between companies |

> **Tip**
>
> Regardless of the strategy selected, an awareness campaign should be utilised to communicate the goals, objectives and key milestones of the project. Similar to a sales and marketing campaign, the awareness campaign should be targeted at the people building, using, or funding the project... in fact, everyone should be aware of the project.

### 4.2.3    Managing trade-offs

Jim McCarthy, the author of *Dynamics of Software Development*, states: 'As a development manager, you're working with only three things: resources (people and money), features (the product or service and its quality), and the schedule. This triangle of elements is all you work with. There is nothing else to be worked with. And changing one side of the triangle has an impact on at least one other side, usually two.'

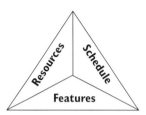

*Figure 4.3 – Project elements in triangulated relationship*

This concept is extremely important in understanding how project variables, and thus delivery strategy, must balance these elements in order to deliver the application or IT service that best responds to the key business drivers. Each delivery strategy described above creates a different set of dynamics among these elements. Thus, it is crucial that the key business drivers be well understood in order to know which delivery strategy will be most effective. If time to market is the key business driver, then features and resources must be adjusted accordingly to meet the schedule required.

It may also be necessary to evaluate several approaches against this triangle to determine which delivery strategy will be optimal for a given project. This in turn means that the delivery strategy chosen may need to be adjusted or even abandoned if a change occurs. It should also be noted that the balance between these project elements at the beginning of a project tends to be somewhat hazy and unclear. It is only through preparing the project scope and definition phases that this balance comes into focus. Many milestones will need to be reached before this picture is completely clear, but generally speaking, the project triangle can be determined with some degree of confidence once the following items have been completed, or are substantially complete:

- key business driver definition
- project objectives and scope (where key business drivers would be described)
- functional specification
- design specification
- project plan.

Each of the above deliverables might take a significant amount of time to complete, which is why initial project estimates for features, resources, and schedule are done with fairly broad ranges for each area. This is often referred to as rough-order-of-magnitude estimates. As the project gains approval through each phase, these estimates are continually refined until a solid project plan is known and can be managed with a relatively high degree of confidence. Project planning is covered in detail in OGC's *Managing Successful Projects with PRINCE2*.

Here is a very simplified example that illustrates the dynamic effects of the triangle. Say a given triangle is defined as having 10 resources to deliver 20 features in 15 weeks. During development, the Customer discovers a new critical feature that is not part of the original feature list in the functional specification. Adding this new feature to the triangle creates an imbalance with the other sides. The team must correct this imbalance by dropping features, increasing resource capacity (adding resources or increasing work hours), changing the schedule, or some combination of all three actions.

The key point is that the trade-offs made between these project elements must be understood and managed or the project will have no hope of being delivered on schedule, on budget, or to the approved functional specification. This is true from preparing the initial project scope all the way through to final production Release.

## 4.3 Preparing to deliver the application

### 4.3.1 Requirements: functional or non-functional?

In typical application development projects, more than 70% of the effort is spent on designing and building generic functions and on satisfying the non-functional requirements (see Section 5.2 for a more detailed discussion on the distinction between functional and non-functional requirements). That is because each individual application needs to provide a solution for such generic features as printing, error handling, and security. The result is that application developers keep doing the same work over and over to meet the needs of non-functional requirements. The more important implication is that developers are spending only 30% of their effort in the analysis, designing, and building of the functional requirements.

Among others, the Object Management Group (OMG, www.omg.com) defined a large number of services that are needed in every application. OMG's object management architecture (OMA) clearly distinguishes between functional and non-functional aspects of an application. It builds on the concept of providing a run time environment that offers all sorts of services to an application.

In this concept, the application covers the functional aspects and the environment covers all non-functional aspects. Application developers should, by definition, focus on the functional aspects of an application, while others can focus on the creation of the environment that provides the necessary non-functional services. This means that the application developers focus on the requirements of the business, while the architecture developers or application framework developers focus on the requirements of the application developers.

### 4.3.2 Architecture, application frameworks and standards

> 'Architecture is often among the first victims felled by today's time-boxed software projects, short release cycles, and rapid application development. There seems to be no time to think through the consequences of architectural decisions.' (Larry Constantine)

Constantine's observation is valid, and offers the solution for the identified problem in the same quote. Architecture-related activities have to be planned and managed separately from software projects. It is also important that architecture-related activities be performed for the benefit of more than just one application. As pointed out in Paragraph 4.3.1 application developers should focus on a single application, while application framework developers should focus on more than one application, and on the common features of those applications, in particular.

The concept of an application framework is a very powerful one. The application framework covers all non-functional aspects and actually provides solutions for all the non-functional requirements that surround an application (see Figure 4.4). The application framework developers should carefully analyse the needs of the application developers and develop application frameworks that address those needs.

A common practice is to distinguish between various types of applications. For instance, not every application can be built on top of a Microsoft ® Windows 2000 platform, connected to a UNIX server, using HTML, Java applets, JavaBeans and a relational database. The various types of applications can be regarded as application families. All applications in the same family are based on the same application framework. And, consequently, every application family has a corresponding application framework.

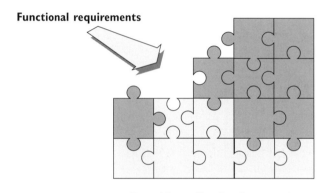

**Functional requirements**

**Reusable application framework,
reflecting non-functional requirements**

*Figure 4.4 – The application framework*

Utilising the concept of an application framework, the first step of the application design phase is to identify the appropriate application framework. If the application framework is mature, a large number of the design decisions are given. If it is not mature, and all non-functional requirements cannot be met on top of an existing application framework, two strategies can be followed.

The first strategy is to collect and analyse the requirements that cannot be dealt with in the current version of the application framework. Based on the application requirements, new requirements can be defined for the application framework. Next, the application framework can be modified so that it can cope with the application requirements. In fact, the whole family of applications that corresponds to the application framework can then use the newly added or changed framework features.

Developing and maintaining an application framework is a complex task, and can be performed by only the most skilled designers in a company. Alternatively, application frameworks can be acquired from third parties. Experience, however, shows that the effort required to tailor such a framework to the company's specific needs is significant and time-consuming. Maintaining the acquired framework, again, demands highly skilled professionals.

The second strategy is to feed the requirements phase with the restrictions imposed by the application framework. Practice shows that it is both feasible and highly beneficial to influence and lead the requirements when they are specified.

### Example

A staffing agency specified the requirements for a new information system supporting the agents. The User interface requirements had been developed in cooperation with a specialised interaction design bureau. The look-and-feel requirements were powerful and heavily supported by the responsible business units. The development organisation decided to define and build an application framework capable of fulfilling these User interface requirements. In fact, the application framework developers developed a User interface kit that could be used by the application developers to create the User interface required. The next Release of the same application, however, started with a requirements phase in which a different view on the nature of the User interface was introduced. Implementing the new view alongside the original view required a compromise that would seriously impact on the quality of the system. The decision was made by the IT organisation to challenge the new User interface requirements and to adjust them in the direction of the original requirements and the corresponding User interface kit. At the end of the discussion only a few modifications to the User interface kit were needed, and the User interface of the application was still regarded as innovative and attractive.

Implied in the use of application frameworks is the concept of standardisation. If an organisation uses and has to maintain an application framework for every single application, there will not be many benefits of the use of an application framework. The benefits will be significantly higher when the number of applications outnumbers the number of application frameworks. In terms of the concept of application families, an organisation should aim for a few large families of application frameworks. Aiming for large families ensures that a large number of applications will reuse the same components to implement the non-functional requirements of the applications. Aiming for a *few* families makes it easier for an organisation to develop and maintain them.

The best approach is for an organisation to standardise on a small number of application frameworks, and ensure that new applications are specified, designed, and built in line with those frameworks.

That, of course, means that an organisation that wants to develop and maintain application frameworks, and to ensure the application frameworks comply with the needs of the application developers, must invest in doing so.

### 4.3.3    Design patterns

The introduction of the new concept of design patterns gave a boost to an organisation's ability to document application frameworks. Design patterns describe both a problem and a solution for common issues encountered during application development. The power of the patterns lies in the fact that the problems they cover are common, while the solutions, on the other hand, leave enough alternatives and room for discussion to significantly improve the knowledge about the problems addressed. In fact, a well-documented design pattern consistently promotes the use of just a small number of design principles.

An important design principle used as the basis for a large number of the design patterns found in recent literature (e.g. *Design patterns, elements of reusable object-oriented software* by Gamma, Helm, Johnson and Vlissides) is that of *separation of concern*. Separation of concerns will lead to applications divided into components with a strong cohesion and minimal coupling between components. The advantage of such an application is that modification can be made to individual components with little or no impact on other components.

# 5 THE APPLICATION MANAGEMENT LIFECYCLE

## 5.1 The application lifecycle

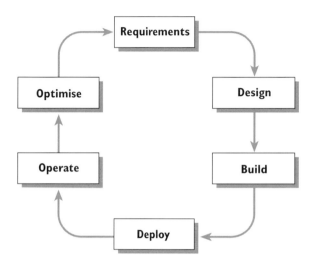

Figure 5.1 – The application lifecycle

Application lifecycle is a term used to describe the various phases through which an application travels from the point at which it is conceived until the point at which it is formally retired. These phases include the traditional application development phases and the Service Management phases, combined into a single lifecycle. Those phases are Requirements, Design, and Build, which constitute the application development portion of the application's lifecycle, and Deploy, Operate, and Optimise, which constitute the Service Management portion of the application's lifecycle.

Although the lifecycle model described seems to be linear and 'waterfall' based, it is perfectly suitable for use in the light of 'modern' system development approaches such as Rapid Application Development (RAD). See Paragraph 5.1.5 for more details.

It is important to note that merely adding features to an existing application, or using it in different ways, does not constitute creating a new application, which means that there is no new application lifecycle. In fact, the lifecycle of any application continues until it is formally ended by retirement.

It is also important to note that an application has not been retired just because it is not in widespread use any longer. An application is retired only when it no longer supports a business function and, even then, will be considered retired only if the application has been purposely removed from the IT environment, meaning that all program files have been removed from the systems involved. If that has not been done, the application still exists, will use resources, and needs to be considered when the IT environment changes.

That is a crucial point. Toward the end of the last century, thousands of work hours were spent preparing applications to make them Y2K ready, although many of the applications no longer supported business functions.

### 5.1.1 Aligning Application Development and Service Management

Although the IT industry has traditionally made a distinction between Application Development (creating a service) and Service Management (delivering the service), that has not always worked well. In fact, it frequently results in a disconnect between the creation of applications and the efforts to maintain them. The Application Management approach to IT sees the two as interrelated parts of a whole, which need to be aligned.

This paragraph focuses on that alignment from the Service Management perspective, with a special emphasis on the importance of dealing early in the lifecycle with those issues that can have a large impact on the effectiveness and efficiency of service delivery.

One important aspect of that overall alignment is the need to align underlying support structures. Application development environments traditionally have their own computer assisted/aided software engineering (CASE) tools that offer the means to specify requirements, draw design diagrams (according to particular modelling standards), or even generate complete applications, or nearly complete application skeletons, almost ready to be deployed. These environments also provide a central location for storing and managing all the elements that are created during application development, generally called a repository. Repository functionality includes version control and consistency checking across various models.

Integration and alignment of those application development tools was given a lot of attention, but little progress was made until the worldwide application development community accepted a *de facto* standard for the syntax of design models, called the unified modelling language (UML). Having a standard modelling language now allows tool vendors to focus on supporting the creation of models instead of focusing on their notation. Also, integration of tools becomes a lot easier, because the syntax used in different tools is now based on one common language, UML.

Like application development environments, Service Management support environments also provide the means to store and manage the elements that are relevant for the execution of Service Management functions. Examples of elements that are stored in such an environment are configuration and dependency specifications, release information, and problem logs. Also in the Service Management arena, initiatives are under way that should lead to standards for specifying information about an application that is required for a management tool to manage the application. Examples (see Section 5.4) include IBM's Application Management Specification (AMS), Microsoft's Windows Management Instrumentation (WMI), and the work from the Distributed Management Task Force (DMTF, www.dmtf.org). The standard, when applied, should provide machine-readable information about the many details that might be undocumented or difficult to locate in the documentation that can be used by management tools.

Examples of the information needed to align service creation and service delivery are:

- application components with their interdependencies
- planning of releases of the application (incremental development)
- directories to locate and store binary files and application-related files, such as help files, required for deployment of the application or redeployment of parts of the application
- scripts to be run before or after deployment
- scripts to start or stop the application
- scripts to check hardware and software configuration of target systems before deployment or installation

- specification of metrics and events that can be retrieved from the application and that indicate the performance status of the application
- customised scripts initiated by the system administrator to manage the application (including the handling of application upgrades)
- specification of access control information for the system resources used by an application
- specification of the details required to track an application's major transactions
- SLA targets and requirements
- operational requirements (allowing the profiling of resources)
- support requirements
- Service Management requirements and targets

In addition to having the information that describes the management-related characteristics of a single application, it is often necessary to define how an application relates to other applications in order to plan completely for the management of the whole application portfolio.

In short, the benefits of an aligned approach are:

- mutual understanding of dependencies that exist between application development and Service Management, leading to balanced design decisions in the earlier phases of the lifecycle
- integral planning of applications, from drawing board to deployment, i.e. application portfolio management, taking into account the Total Cost of Ownership (TCO)
- an integral view on TCO, allowing the IT department to be more precise and more accurate in linking IT costs to business benefits
- capacity requirements available early in the cycle, allowing infrastructure capacity planning aligned with applications 'in the pipeline'
- development, test, and production environments that can be managed in a well-coordinated way, lowering cost for defining, building, changing, and removing these environments
- reference architectures and/or frameworks that can be developed to take into account issues for service creation (such as time to market) and service delivery (such as availability)
- application development project managers and service managers who have a common ground on which they can define cross-phase performance indicators that can be monitored and followed up
- application designers who can design for functionality specifically aimed at Service Management; in fact, they could design applications that are 'management ready'.

### 5.1.2 Implementation of the application lifecycle in the organisation

The majority of readers of this book will fulfil one or more roles in the service delivery organisation. Therefore this book can help to create a great level of understanding and respect within Service Management and ICT infrastructure management staff about the issues application developers deal with when creating a service. An effective IT organisation, however, also requires application developers to have a significant level of understanding about the impact of decisions made on the delivery of services.

The implication of this is that application development and Service Management departments need to cooperate closely to ensure that every phase in the lifecycle dedicates the appropriate attention to service creation and service delivery aspects.

Best practices show that the alignment of service creation and service delivery can take a long time and has to be executed as an organisational change effort. Experience shows that it has many pitfalls.

### 5.1.3 Phases in the lifecycle

There are a variety of perspectives on the Application Management lifecycle, but they all tend to fall into one of two camps – they either emphasise application development or they emphasise Service Management. The application development perspective distinguishes between global design and detailed design, between unit test and system test, and ends with a very general phase called *maintenance*. The Service Management perspective tends to start with an already developed application, ready to be installed and to be taken into operations.

What is neglected in both views of the application lifecycle is that application development and Service Management in reality have a much tighter relationship than is suggested by the respective lifecycle models.

This book focuses on the application lifecycle from both perspectives (as shown in Figure 5.1), which stresses the need for alignment between both views in every single phase. Those six phases, which combine the phases of application development and Service Management, are as follows:

Requirements

This is the phase during which the requirements for a new application are gathered, based on the business needs of the organisation. It is important to note that there are three types of requirements for any application – functional requirements, non-functional requirements, and usability requirements.

Functional requirements are those specifically required to support a particular business function. Non-functional requirements, looked at from a Service Management perspective, address the need for a responsive, available and secure service, and deal with such issues as deployment, operations, system management and security. Usability requirements are those that address the needs of the End User, and result in features of the system that facilitate its ease of use.

Design

This is the phase during which requirements are translated into feature specifications. The goal for application designs should be satisfying the organisation's requirements. Design includes the design of the application itself, and the design of the environment, or *operational model*, that the application has to run on. Architectural considerations are the most important aspect of this phase, since they can impact on the structure and content of both application and operational model. Architectural considerations for the application (design of the *application architecture*) and architectural considerations for the operation model (design of the *system architecture*) are strongly related and need to be aligned.

Build

In the build phase, both the application and the operational model are made ready for deployment. Application components are coded or acquired, integrated, and tested. Often the distinction is made between a development and test environment. The test environment allows for testing the combination of application and operational model.

Deploy

In this phase, both the operational model and the application are deployed. The operational model is incorporated in the existing IT environment and the application is installed on top of the operational model, using the deployment processes described within ITIL *ICT Infrastructure Management*.

Operate

In the operate phase, the IT services organisation delivers the service required by the business. The performance of the service is measured continually against the Service Levels and key business drivers.

Optimise

In the optimise phase, the results of the Service Level performance measurements are analysed and acted upon. Possible improvements are discussed and developments initiated if necessary. The two main strategies in this phase are to maintain and/or improve the Service Levels and to lower cost. This could lead to another iteration in the lifecycle or to justified retirement of an application.

### 5.1.4    Traversing the lifecycle

One important thing to remember about the application lifecycle is that, because it is circular, the same application can reside in different phases of the lifecycle at the same time. For example, when the next version of an application is being designed, and the current version is deployed, the previous version might still be in operation in parts of an organisation. This obviously requires strong version, configuration and release control (see other ITIL books).

Particular phases might take longer or seem more significant than others, but they are all crucial. Every application must go through all of them at least once, and, because of the circular nature of the lifecycle, will go through some more than once.

Good communication is the key as an application works its way through the phases of the lifecycle. It is critical that high quality information is passed along by those handling the application in one phase of its existence to those handling it in the next phase. It is also important that an organisation monitors the quality of the Application Management lifecycle. Changes in the lifecycle, for example, in the way an organisation passes information between the different phases, will affect its quality. Understanding the characteristics of every phase in the Application Management lifecycle is crucial to improving the quality of the whole. Methods and tools used in one phase might have an impact on others, while optimisation of one phase might sub-optimise the whole.

### 5.1.5 Alternative lifecycle models

The application lifecycle model described here can also be viewed as linear, and 'waterfall' based, and is therefore perfectly suitable for use in the light of 'modern' system development approaches such as Rapid Application Development (RAD). Most 'modern' variations on the traditional waterfall approach introduce increments and iterations in the development process.

The main reason for the introduction of increments and iterations in the development process is management of the risks associated with uncertainty and changing requirements. Still, every business function of the application needs to be understood (requirements phase), designed and built.

The use of increments implies that a system is developed piece by piece. Every piece could support one of the business functions that the entire system needs to support. Incremental delivery could result in shorter time to market for specific business functions. The development of every increment requires traversal of the entire lifecycle.

Iterative development implies that the lifecycle will be traversed more than once, by design. A development team can decide to focus first on those elements of the application that are most clear (or unclear) or are most important for the business. One can also decide to use techniques such as prototyping to get a better understanding of the requirements (by testing non-functional behaviour and through communication with business Users). After the prototype has been designed and built, the prototype is deployed in the prototype environment, carefully operated for a while, and then thrown away (retired) or extended or modified to better support the requirements.

Endless combinations of iterative and incremental approaches are possible. One can, for instance, start with the specification of requirements for the entire system, followed by the design and build of the application per increment. However, at the end, for every application increment developed, none of the lifecycle phases can be skipped.

## 5.2 Requirements

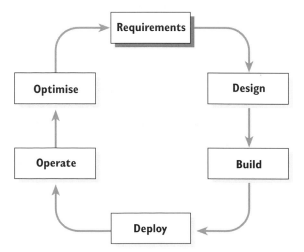

### 5.2.1 Overview

All applications start their journey through the application lifecycle in the requirements phase. This is the phase during which the development team works closely with key business decision-makers to determine the organisation's requirements for the application. The requirements phase identifies the functionality, performance levels, and other characteristics that the application must satisfy. The requirements developed in this phase serve as a foundation for the remaining phases of the development process, and as the acceptance criteria. NB: Requirements for modification of an existing application may originate from the optimise phase in the form of a Request For Change (RFC).

There are three types of requirements for decision-makers to consider – functional requirements, non-functional requirements, and usability requirements.

### 5.2.2    Functional requirements

Functional requirements describe the things an application is intended to do, and can be expressed as services, tasks or functions the application is required to perform.

One approach for specifying functional requirements is through such methods as a system context diagram or a use case model.

A system context diagram, for instance, captures all information exchanges between, on the one hand, the application system and its environment, and, on the other, sources or destinations of data used by the application. These information exchanges and data sources represent constraints on the application under development.

A use case model defines a goal-oriented set of interactions between external actors and the system under consideration. Actors are parties outside the system that interact with the system. An actor may be a class of Users, roles Users can play, or other systems. The main purpose of use case modelling is to establish the boundary of the proposed application and fully state the functional capabilities to be delivered to the Users. Use cases are also helpful for establishing or enforcing communication between business and application developers. They provide a basis for sizing and planning the development effort, and feed the definition of usability requirements.

Recent developments show that use cases are used to cover the functional aspects of Service Level Agreements (SLAs). Practice has shown that use cases can be used throughout the lifecycle for testing purposes. Use cases define all scenarios that an application has to support, and can therefore easily be expanded into test cases. Since use cases describe an application's functionality on a level that's understandable for both business and IT, they can serve as a vehicle to specify the functional elements of an SLA.

One level 'below' the use case and the context diagram, many other modelling techniques can be applied. These models depict the static and dynamic characteristics of the application under development. A conceptual data model (whether called object, data or component model) describes the different components in the system, their mutual relationships and their internal structure. Dynamics of the applications can be described using state models (e.g. state transition diagrams) that show the various states of the system together with events that may cause state changes. Interactions between the different application components can be described using interaction diagrams (e.g. object interaction diagrams). Besides a mature requirements modelling process, CASE tools can help in getting and keeping these models consistent, correct and complete.

### 5.2.3    Non-functional requirements

Non-functional requirements are used to define requirements and constraints on the IT system.

The requirements serve as a basis for early system sizing and estimates of cost, and can support the assessment of the viability of the proposed IT system.

Most importantly, they drive design of the operational models. Non-functional requirements are frequently the most important determining factor of the architecture. Two systems with the same use cases but with very different non-functional requirements need very different designs or architectures.

Non-functional requirements should also encourage application developers to take a broader view of project goals, because they often refer to global rather than local properties of the software.

Categories of non-functional requirements are:

- Manageability (Does it run? Does it fail? How does it fail?)
- Efficiency (How many resources does it consume?)
- Effectiveness (IT is doing the right things and IT understands business goals and provides effective input to business planning process)
- Inter-operability – inter-working with other applications and services
- Availability and reliability (How reliable does it need to be?)
- Capacity and performance
- Security
- Correctability (How quickly can it be recovered after failure? Are there recovery procedures/tools?)
- Installability (How much effort does it take to install the application? Is it using automated install procedures?)
- Controllability (Does it have standardised configurations? Is there predictability of demand?)
- Maintainability (How well can the application be adjusted?)
- Operability (Do the applications disturb other applications in their functionalities?)
- Securability (Are applications secure from interference from outside the designated User community?).

The non-functional requirements can be used to prescribe the quality attributes of the application being built. These quality attributes can be used to design test plans for testing the applications on the compliance to non-functional requirements. See Chapter 7.

### 5.2.4    Usability requirements

The primary purpose of usability requirements is to ensure that the system meets the expectations of its Users with regard to its ease of use. The work product is used to:

- provide baseline guidance to the User interface developers on User interface design
- establish performance standards for usability evaluations
- define test scenarios for usability test plans and usability testing.

Like the non-functional requirements, usability requirements can also be used as the quality attributes of design test plans for testing the applications on the compliance to usability requirements. Quality attributes and testing are expanded further in Chapter 7.

### 5.2.5    Change cases

An important new development in the area of requirements is the specification of change cases. Change cases specify changes to the application's functionality that are likely to be required in the future. As with other requirements documents, change cases are used to clarify scope and direction with the sponsor. Extra architecture and design work will be needed at this point to ensure the change cases can be met in the future at reasonable cost. The sponsor must be prepared to pay the extra cost. If not, the change cases should be reduced to what the sponsor is prepared to pay for. Change cases are also used to evaluate the architecture. They influence the development process enabling the design of appropriate architectural features to minimise the impact of future changes.

In line with Section 4.3, application framework developers will often consider change cases. In a sense, change cases specify the flexibility that is required to support likely future demands.

### 5.2.6    Testing requirements

Testing of requirements is an often-overlooked possibility to improve significantly the quality of the application under development. Techniques that can be used include prototyping (to test both functional and non-functional requirements), User interface mock-ups, 'sticky wall reviews' (a technique where models printed on paper are stuck on a wall, allowing peer reviewers to comment and question), document reviews, presentations, etc.

The challenge with testing requirements at this stage is that the amount of requirements can be very large and no overview exists. Another challenge to overcome is the fact that many stakeholders (application owners, Users, requirement modellers themselves) might have different assumptions and opinions on what the system has to deliver. Any technique or tool adding clarity and overview, and facilitating a discussion, will help in improving the quality of the requirement models. Every misunderstanding that can be avoided at this stage pays off later in time and in quality.

### 5.2.7    Requirements management checklist

When identifying the requirements for an application it is important that all the Service Management functions are fully considered and addressed within the requirements phase. Table 5.1 provides examples of manageability checks for this phase.

*Table 5.1 – Management checklist for the requirements phase*

| *Service Management functions* | *Examples of requirements phase manageability checks* |
| --- | --- |
| Configuration Management | Identify environment that application will need to run on |
| Change Management | Specify change cases<br>Specify the level of changes that the application can accommodate (part/whole etc.) |
| Release Management | Identify how applications need to be released, including what makes up a Release<br>Identify how the Release relates to the Releases of other applications<br>Note that a Release can be driven by business requirement or other |

| Service Management functions | Examples of requirements phase manageability checks |
|---|---|
| Security Management | What are the security requirements that the application needs to satisfy? |
| Incident Management | Identify how to handle errors in the application<br>Identify corporate standard for error handling, and consider implementing one if there is none<br>Identify how to handle errors in the organisation |
| Problem Management | Understand the Problem Management process used in the environment |
| Capacity Management | Understand the capacity capabilities that will be available within the environment<br>Understand the capacity required for the solution (hardware, network etc.) |
| Availability Management | Determine how available the business needs the application to be<br>Determine whether the requirement is 7 x 24 x 365 |
| Service Continuity Management | Determine how long the business can operate without the service<br>Determine how the business will operate without the service |
| Service Level Management | Identify what level of service the business needs |
| Financial Management | Identify the financial case for the application<br>Determine how this application contributes to the business and how value and costs are managed<br>Identify who pays for the application – development and ongoing costs (operation and maintenance) |

### 5.2.8 Organisation of the requirements team

The requirements team will require representation from a number of the key Service Management areas to ensure that it completes its activities comprehensively. Each role can be fulfilled by one or more people and would include:

- Change and Configuration Management (CCM)
- support
- operations
- security
- ICT infrastructure management.

Change and Configuration Management (CCM)

The Change and Configuration Management role is responsible for Change, Release, and Configuration Management, which are the main processes involved in moving the application from the development environment into live production use. The CCM role owns the Configuration Management Database (CMDB), which is widely used throughout the whole application lifecycle. The CCM is also the owner of Change Management and therefore is critical in the whole approval process for changes made to the application. In this phase, the CCM provides information that defines the Change, configuration, and Release requirements for the application. More detail on the processes involved can be found in ITIL *Service Support*.

## Support

The support role is responsible for the supportability of the application including Incident and Problem Management. This role would help define the requirements that relate to how the application will be supported once it is in live use and how the service can be restored as fast as possible. Incident and Problem Management are also covered in detail in ITIL *Service Support*.

## Operations

The operations role is responsible for the day-to-day activities for maintaining the application once it moves from development to live usage. This role will help define the operational requirements of the application, to ensure that the ongoing maintenance of the application is defined and planned in a manner compatible with other applications in use in the organisation. Requirements standards for daily, weekly, monthly, and ad hoc maintenance tasks fall within the responsibility of this role.

## Security

The security role plays an important part in nearly all IT activities, especially in e-business. An information system with a weak security foundation will eventually be breached. Depending on the information system and the severity of the breach, the results could vary from embarrassment, to loss of data, to loss of revenue, to loss of life. In effect, the security role actively practises Risk Management in all activities that it performs. The primary goals of the security role are to ensure:

- **Data confidentiality.** No one should be able to view data unless authorised to do so
- **Data integrity.** All authorised Users should feel confident that the data presented to them is accurate and not improperly modified
- **Data availability.** Authorised Users should be able to access the data they need, when and where they need it. This can be a particular issue for mobile working.

Another responsibility of the IT security role is creation of a comprehensive plan for the audit, retention, classification, and secure disposal of data. Legal, financial, and historical data need to be safely stored for appropriate periods of time as defined by law, the industry, and the corporation. Non-critical data should be disposed of to minimise the cost of expensive storage. This requires implementing an efficient backup and retrieval process in the operations role. Physical security, as it relates to data, assures secure telephone and data connections and physical access to assets, as well as securing connections to business partners, joint ventures, and new acquisitions. Exposures related to weak physical security allow easy access to intruders.

## ICT infrastructure management

The ICT infrastructure management role looks at the evolving enterprise architecture and ensures that plans are in place to meet the new and changing requirements of running the business from a networking, telecommunications, hardware, and software perspective.

Responsibilities such as defining requirements for capacity and availability management fall within the purview of this role in this phase. Identification of SLA requirements will also involve this role. For more information see ITIL *Service Delivery*, and *ICT Infrastructure Management*.

## 5.3    Design

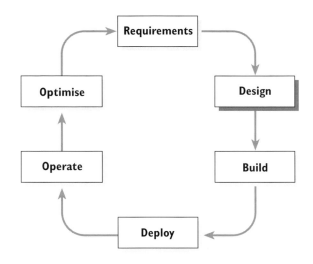

### 5.3.1    Overview

The design phase is one of the most important phases within the application lifecycle. It ensures that an application is conceived with operability and Application Management in mind. This phase takes the outputs from the requirements phase and turns them into the specification that will be used to build the application.

It is widely accepted that the later one makes a change within the lifecycle of an application, the harder and more expensive it is to implement this change successfully. For instance, compare application development to the work needed to build a house. Changes made while the house is being designed are easy to accommodate compared with changes that are introduced once construction work starts. Moving a doorway at the start of the design phase involves redoing some drawings and possibly some calculations. Moving the door once the house is built might involve such major structural activities as rebuilding a wall.

Generally, in the design phase, the same models will be produced as have been delivered in the requirements phase, but during design many more details are added. New models include the architecture models, where the way in which the different functional components are mapped to the physical components (e.g. desktops, servers, databases and network) needs to be defined. The mapping, together with the estimated load of the system, should allow for the sizing of the infrastructure required.

Another important aspect of the architecture model is the embedding of the application in the existing environment. Which pieces of the existing infrastructure will be used to support the required new functions? Can existing servers or networks be used? With what impact? Are required functions available in existing applications that can be utilised? Do packages exist that offer the functionality needed or should the functions be built from scratch?

There is an obvious need to document those characteristics of the system that need to be known for proper deployment and operation of the applications. However, this is often ignored or neglected.

The design phase takes all requirements into consideration and starts assembling them into an initial design for the solution. Doing this not only gives developers a basis to begin working: it is also likely to bring up questions that need to be asked of the Customers. If possible, application frameworks should be applied (see Section 4.3) as a starting point.

It is not always possible to foresee every aspect of a solution's design ahead of time. As a solution is developed, new things will be learned about how to do things and also how not to. Encountering unplanned obstacles often requires refining an understanding of the Customer's needs.

The key is to create a flexible design, so that making a change does not send developers all the way back to the beginning of the design phase. There are a number of approaches that can minimise the chance of this happening, including:

- designing for non-functional requirements/manageability
- using risk-driven scheduling techniques
- managing trade-offs
- using application-independent design guidelines; using application frameworks
- employing a structured design process/manageability checklist
- organising the design team roles.

### 5.3.2    Design for non-functional requirements/manageability

Design for non-functional requirements means giving non-functional requirements a level of importance similar to that for the functional requirements, and including them as a mandatory part of the design phase. This includes a number of non-functional requirements such as availability, maintainability, and reliability. It is now inconceivable in modern application development projects that User interface design (usability requirements) would be omitted as a key design activity. However, many organisations ignore or forget manageability.

### 5.3.3    Risk-driven scheduling

Risk-driven scheduling assigns higher-risk tasks a high priority and includes risk priorities that are assigned to meet Customer requirements. This means that the highest risk activities are done first, so that if something goes wrong or does not happen in the way it was planned, there is more time to recover and impact on the critical path of the project is avoided.

### 5.3.4    Managing trade-offs

Managing trade-off decisions focuses on balancing the relationship among resources, the project schedule, and those features that need to be included in the application for the sake of quality.

When development teams try to complete this balancing, it is often at the expense of the non-functional requirements. One way to avoid that is to include non-functional requirements in the application-independent design guidelines, for example in the form of an application framework. For a full description of managing trade-offs see Paragraph 4.2.3.

### 5.3.5 Application-independent design guidelines and application frameworks

The use of application-independent design guidelines promotes manageability within a development, by allowing development teams to include non-functional requirements by default in the design process. Operability and manageability effectively become standard components of all design processes, for example, in the form of an application framework (see Section 4.3), and get embedded into the working practices and culture of the development organisation. See Appendix B for a detailed table of design guidelines.

### 5.3.6 Design management checklist

Organisations need a process that allows for testing the design against the high-level functional requirements for the organisation and any special non-functional requirements that have been identified for the application. The testing process should consider all the main ITIL Service Management functions and review how the design supports them. Table 5.2 provides examples of manageability checks for the design phase.

*Table 5.2 – Management checklist for the design phase*

| *Service Management functions* | *Examples of design phase manageability checks* |
| --- | --- |
| Configuration Management | Are the designers aware of the corporate standards used for Configuration Management? How does the design meet organisational standards for acceptable configurations? Does the design support the concept of version control? Is the design created in a way that allows for the logical breakdown of the application into Configuration Items (CIs)? |
| Change Management | Does the application design cope with change? Do the designers understand the Change Management process used by the organisation? |
| Release Management | Do the application designers understand the standards and tools used for releasing applications into the environment? How will the design ensure that this application can be released into the environment in a simple and efficient way? |
| Security Management | How does the design ensure that the application is designed with security in the forefront? |
| Incident Management | Does the design facilitate simple creation of Incidents when something goes wrong? Is the design compatible with the organisational Incident Management system? Does the design accommodate automatic logging and detection of Incidents? |
| Problem Management | How does the design facilitate the methods used for root cause analysis used within the organisation? |

| Capacity Management | Are the designers aware of the approach to capacity management used within the organisation? How to measure operations and performance? Is modelling being used to ensure that the design meets capacity needs? |
|---|---|
| Availability Management | Does the design address the availability requirements of the application? Has the application been designed to fit in with backup and recovery capabilities of the organisation? |
| Service Continuity Management | How does the design meet the service continuity requirements of the organisation? Will the design meet the needs of the business recovery process following a disaster? |
| Service Level Management | How does the design meet the SLA requirements of the organisation? |
| Financial Management | Does the design meet the financial requirements for this application? How does the design ensure that the final application will meet return of investment expectations? |

### 5.3.7 Problems with design guidelines

During the design phase, designers should identify where the design guidelines fail to cover the non-functional requirements. It is important that these get fed back into the design process both by updating the application and by modifying the overall design guidelines and application frameworks so that they are reflected in future application developments.

### 5.3.8 Testing the requirements

Just as the functional and non-functional requirements for an application should be documented and properly specified, so should the design actions needed to comply with the functional requirements. This enables the test team to verify, using static testing, whether the design properly addresses the application's functional and non-functional requirements. Several techniques can be used to verify the compliance to the functional and non-functional requirements. Examples of these are:

- **Inspection:** the most formal review method and rigorous form of static testing – a well-defined and understood procedure involving planning, overview preparation, inspection meeting, rework, and follow-up
- **Desk check:** the least formal process – a product author reads his or her own work to identify defects
- **Walk-through:** a reading and/or visual inspection of a work product by one or more people in addition to the author
- **Review:** a process used extensively to provide the project with control, quality assurance, and focus on issues affecting the product, the development process, and the

project. A review deals with the characteristics of what is being built, how it is built, and the resources used to build it.

The static tests can be designed after the requirements phase, during the design phase. Static testing should be done before the formal approval of the design. Formal stakeholder approval of the designs, involving such stakeholders as business decision-makers and the IT services organisation, should be based on the static test results.

### 5.3.9  Organisation of the design team

As is the case with the requirements team, the design team needs representation from the same key areas within the Service Management team in order to do its job effectively. Other than the regular application development roles that one would expect on a design team (such as designers of database schemas, User interface, architecture and tests), a number of the key Service Management roles are needed so that Application Management and Operations are fully involved in the important decisions that are taken during design. The outcome of the involvement needs to be reflected in documentation.

These roles can be filled by one or more people and include:

#### Change and Configuration Management

The Change and Configuration Management (CCM) role within the design phase advises the development team on how the application can move from development/test to the live production environment. The role provides expertise on ongoing identification, Change Control, and status reporting of the application. It also consults on version control, software distribution, licence tracking, usage monitoring, and retirement information.

The CCM role also provides expert advice on how the design should provide accessibility to application Configuration Management information so that it can be incorporated into the CMDB. This can be achieved by following a standard for application instrumentation (such as WMI or Desktop Management Instrumentation (DMI)). This would mean that the application has the potential to be automatically inventoried and placed in the CMDB without any operator intervention.

#### Support

The support role within the design phase advises on how a new application's design should facilitate its supportability. That advice includes such things as simplifying access to accurate information for the Service Desk, and direct support for Incident and Problem Management functions. Another responsibility is automatic logging of critical information in a common format, and directing the designers to include a key feature that speeds fail-over/recovery and minimises support costs. One of the other key contributions that the support role can make is to include advance self-help features into the application.

#### Operations

The operations role in the design phase focuses on ensuring that the day-to-day system tasks the application will need to be run and controlled effectively are fully considered throughout design. This should include how the application's operational aspects will potentially integrate into the operation model and could contain a number of the following aspects:

- Designing the application so that its operational controls are consistent with the controls of other applications and infrastructure systems, and so that these operational controls automatically publish themselves into a systems management console
- Designing scheduled and repeatable processes, such as data backup, archiving and storage, output management, system monitoring and event log management, so that they follow the same organisation-wide operation management standards
- Considering Operational Level Agreements (OLAs) and ensuring that the design is completed to support both these and the overall SLA
- Ensuring that the design of the operational documentation of an application fits in with and follows standards that the entire organisation uses for this type of documentation.

### Security

Security Management within the design phase focuses on ensuring that the application is designed to meet the security requirements of the organisation. Specifically, this means ensuring that the application support is designed to facilitate a number of the security requirements, so that it:

- assists in monitoring correct operations of IT resources
- supports intrusion detection and virus protection
- is not susceptible to denial of service
- supports group standards and policies for data retention and secure data disposal
- includes data for use in audit tracking and reporting
- works with network domain security design and management
- is not vulnerable to network attacks
- provides alerts to help with real-time network intrusion responses
- supports appropriate security technology requirements
- supports the organisation's User policies and requirements (e.g. password policy)
- meets external and physical security requirements (e.g. access to computer rooms)
- includes secure messaging requirements.

### ICT infrastructure management

The ICT infrastructure management role in the design phase is involved in a number of areas, including capacity, availability, and service continuity management. Application developers need to consider each of these areas during the design phase and ensure that the design and the subsequent Application Management handle the following:

- forecasting and capacity management of both the applications and the underlying infrastructure that it uses
- monitoring availability of infrastructure services
- providing cost management and budgeting for IT Infrastructure expenses and allocations
- providing server builds, standard images, and software installations

■ providing cost and charge back reporting to management and Customers based on established costing/charging policies.

> **Tip**
>
> **Good practice here is that no design can be signed off without the involvement and approval of all of the above roles.**

| 5.4 | Build |

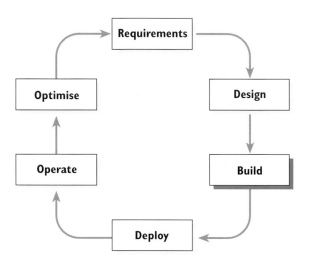

### 5.4.1    Overview

Once the design phase is completed, the application development team will take the designs that have been produced and move on to building and testing the application. To ensure that the application is built with management at the core, the development team needs to focus on ensuring that the building phase continues to correctly address the non-functional aspects of the design (responsiveness, availability, security).

The build phase covers the following topics:

■ consistent coding conventions

■ application-independent building guidelines

■ operability testing

■ management checklist for the building phase

■ organisation of the build team roles.

### 5.4.2    Consistent coding conventions

The main reason for using a consistent set of design and coding conventions is to standardise the structure and coding style of an application so that everyone can easily read, understand, and manage the application development process. Good design and coding conventions result in precise, readable, and unambiguous source code that is consistent with the organisational coding and management standards, and is as intuitive to follow as possible. Adding application operability into this convention ensures that all applications are built in a way that ensures that they can be fully managed all the way through their lifecycles.

A general-purpose set of conventions should define the minimum requirements necessary to accomplish the purposes discussed above, leaving the programmer free to create the program's logic and functional flow. The object is to make the program easy to manage and operate without cramping the programmer's natural creativity with excessive constraints and arbitrary restrictions.

A coding convention itself can be a significant aid to managing the application, as consistency allows the management tools to interact with the application in a known way. It is better to introduce a minimum set of conventions that everyone will follow rather than to create an overly complex set that encompasses every facet but is not followed or used consistently across the organisation.

### 5.4.3 Application-independent building guidelines

#### Templates, code generation, and application frameworks

A number of development tools provide a variety of templates for creating common application components. Rather than creating all the pieces of an application from scratch, developers can customise an existing template. They can also reuse custom components in multiple applications by creating their own templates.

Other development tools will generate large pieces of code (skeletons) based on the design models and coding conventions. The code could include hooks at the code pieces that need to be added.

Section 4.2 discusses the use of application frameworks. Application frameworks can cover many of the non-functional requirements in a way that is standard among a number of applications with similar characteristics.

In this respect, templates and application frameworks should be considered assets. These assets not only guide the building of applications, but also incorporate the lessons learned or intellectual capital from previous application development efforts. The more that standard components are designed into the solution, the faster applications can be developed, against lower costs in the long term (not ignoring the fact that development of templates, code generators, and application frameworks requires significant investment).

#### Embedded application instrumentation

The application design phase introduced the concept of embedded application instrumentation. The build phase deals with incorporating the instrumentation into the fabric of the application.

Developers need a consistent way to provide instrumentation for application drivers (e.g. database drivers) and applications, that is efficient and easy to implement. To keep application developers from reinventing the wheel with every new application they develop, the computer industry provides methods and technologies to simplify and facilitate the instrumentation process. These include:

- IBM Application Management Specification (AMS)
- Distributed Management Task Force (DMTF)
- Desktop Management Instrumentation (DMI)

■ Microsoft Windows© Management Instrumentation (WMI).

Each of these technologies provides a consistent and richly descriptive model of the configuration, status, and operational aspects of applications and systems. These are provided through programming Application Program Interfaces (APIs) that the developer incorporates into an application, normally through the use of standard programming templates.

It is important to ensure that all applications are built to conform to some level of compliance for the application instrumentation. Ways in which to do this could include:

■ Provide access to management data through the instrumentation API

If the application uses management functions and data provided by the system and/or other products, and that data is available through the instrumentation namespace, it should use the instrumentation API to access that management information rather than native APIs. This would normally include various management objects, performance monitor, and event log data. The instrumentation API allows for greater interoperability of applications and management information.

An example of this is Microsoft's Windows Management Instrumentation. This is a technology that provides a common framework to instrument an application so that it is possible to perform activities such as end-to-end monitoring or performance.

■ Publish management data to other management systems, again through the instrumentation API

If the application has management functions and data that permit control or monitoring of the application by other management applications, it should be exposed through the instrumentation API. If the application generates events, these should also be forwarded via the instrumentation API to the management application that processes them.

■ Conform to the rules for extending the common namespace

This means that the embedded application instrumentation is described in a way that not only the developer of the application understands, but also that other developers/vendors use, so that all applications can coexist and inter-operate. It would be difficult for two systems to work together if they named the object using different methods that are inconsistent and unknown to each other. That would create a high potential for failure.

A number of good sources of information on application instrumentation exist on the Internet. They include:
www.dmtf.org
www.ibm.com
www.microsoft.com

■ Provide application events handling

An application event is a specific action that usually requires some follow-up action. This could be as simple as recording the fact that this event occurred, to something as complex as alerting the security team that someone is trying to break into the system.

Creating, handling, and reporting events both within and across applications is key to understanding what the application is doing and how it is performing.

Managing an application requires an understanding of what it is doing. Producing events that are examined and acted upon by system management tools is central to creating an understandable and predictable system.

- Provide a diagnostic hook

  A diagnostic hook allows a monitoring or debugging tool to spy on the execution of a distributed system and gather diagnostic information. Diagnostic hooks typically provide information about application performance, error conditions, and configuration settings.

  Diagnostic hooks are primarily implemented to increase system availability and reliability. Errors will eventually occur, and diagnostic hooks help minimise application downtime. Good diagnostic hooks help identify the causes of errors and provide information necessary to troubleshoot problems.

  Diagnostic hooks also improve the overall quality of applications. Judiciously recording all errors and using diagnostic hooks to determine the causes of these errors continually improves the quality of an application.

  **Tip**

  **Good practice is to build in diagnostic hooks that can be turned on or off, so that, if something goes wrong in testing or live production use, it is relatively simple to obtain key information that would help diagnose the problem.**

Diagnostic hooks can be divided into three broad categories:

- system level information provided by the OS and hardware
- software level information provided by application infrastructure components such as database, web server, or messaging system
- custom information provided by applications.

Diagnostic hooks are of greatest value during testing and when an error has been discovered in the production system. Diagnostic hooks provide the information necessary to solve problems and application errors.

Errors happen even in applications that have been thoroughly tested. During development, it is impossible for a developer to think of the causes of every possible error and write code accordingly. Eventually, every application, no matter how mission-critical or well developed, will experience errors.

Errors may be caused by something as simple as a change in traffic volumes or usage patterns. Hardware failures of an individual server or failed network components may also produce application errors.

Environmental changes are a huge source of errors. These errors are caused by system changes being rolled into production. Seemingly simple changes to a system component can have far-reaching impact on running applications. Additionally, database schema changes are constantly introduced by business changes and the deployment of new systems. Applications are sometimes prevented from accessing resources because of security changes.

### 5.4.4    Operability testing

As the application is built, it needs to be thoroughly tested to ensure that it meets all the stated requirements and features that the business has requested. Non-functional requirements should be tested as well, in a manner similar to the way basic functionality is tested.

The approach to testing can largely dictate the overall quality of the application when it ships. All too often testing is delayed to the end of the building phase just prior to deployment, and, if the development project has not run true to schedule (as is frequently the case), testing can be rushed or cut short and the overall quality of the deliverable made to suffer.

Quality should be built into an application development project from the start, and the working practices and culture of the development team should include testing as an integral and obligatory activity undertaken at every stage of the project.

Testing of non-functional requirements is a key area of testing that is often overlooked. Any test plan should contain a section that describes each of the non-functional requirements, which area of operability the requirement covers, and how it will be tested. An example of such a requirement could be the requirement that, in a disaster situation, the system can be replaced with a new system and the system state can be restored within eight hours.

Several types of tests are appropriate, including tests that are managed by the development team, such as unit testing, system testing, and integration testing, and tests managed mostly by a separate test team or by the accepting parties, such as functional acceptance testing, User acceptance testing and production acceptance testing. Not until the production acceptance testing activity are most of the non-functional requirements dynamically tested, if they are tested at all. However, in order to ensure high-quality delivery of applications to the deployment phase, testing should be an all-pervasive activity throughout the build phase. Also, just as the requirements could be used as a test basis for testing the work products of the design phase, the work products of the design phase can be used as a test basis for the build phase.

Based on the design of the applications, the test team can build the test plans and test scripts for the tests to be performed. Internal design specifications can be used for unit and system testing, while the external designs can be used to develop acceptance test plans. More details on testing are given in Chapter 7. An example of a unit test plan is shown in Figure 5.2.

As an application goes through several iterations or versions, it should be retested against the original test pack. Such regression testing is the only way to ensure that a bug is not introduced into an area of the application that was previously developed and tested, which can happen in a variety of ways. For example, a change in the way that an application identifies itself to the Configuration Management system might have an impact on Release Management and Incident Management. The reuse of test scripts for regression testing is an essential and integral part of building the test environment.

Another way to ensure that the test environment provides a true reflection of the live production environment is to place it under complete Change and Configuration Management as if it were the live system. This is only applicable if the new application does not require changes to the current live environment. Doing this greatly increases the chances that tests will perform in a manner similar to that of the live environment.

The testing method that is used needs to accommodate the testing of non-functional requirements for the application. This would include as a minimum the areas identified in the build management checklist.

**Project Number:** ........................................................................................................................................

**Project Name:** ...........................................................................................................................................

# UT/LT Test Plan

**For Approval**                                  **For Information**

Issued for: .......... Approval/Information ..............................................................................................

Version: .......... VI.0 ...........................................................................................................................

Issue Date: ..........................................................................................................................................

Author: ...............................................................................................................................................

Telephone: .........................................................................................................................................

IT Manager: .................................................................... Date: ....................................................

Analyst: ........................................................................... Date: ....................................................

Test Unit: ........................................................................ Date: ....................................................

Approvals: Please sign, date and return the Approval Form by **Date** ....................................

Comments: Please use the enclosed Comments Form and return by **Date** ...........................

**If your Approval/Comments have not been received by that date, Approval/No Comment
will be implied.**

**TABLE OF CONTENTS**

*Figure 5.2 – Example of a unit test plan Table of Contents*

### 5.4.5    Build management checklist

The application should be built to meet, and be tested against, the high-level requirements for the organisation and any special management requirements that have been identified for the application. The testing process should consider all the main ITIL Service Management functions and review how the design supports these. Table 5.3 provides examples of manageability checks for the build phase.

*Table 5.3 – Management checklist for the build phase*

| Service Management functions | Examples of build phase manageability checks |
| --- | --- |
| Configuration Management | Have the developers built the application to conform to the corporate standards that are used for Configuration Management? Does the application use only programs and tools that are considered acceptable and are included within the product catalogue? Does the application include support for version control and management? Have the developers built in the chosen CI structure to the application? |
| Change Management | Has the application been built and tested against the corporate Change Management process? |
| Release Management | Has the application been built and tested in ways that ensure it can be released into the environment in a simple and efficient way? |
| Security Management | Is the build process following security best practice for this activity? |
| Incident Management | Is a simple creation-of-Incidents process, for when something goes wrong, built into the application and tested? Has the compatibility with the organisational Incident management system been tested? |
| Problem Management | Has the program's ability to provide information to facilitate root cause analysis and Problem Management been tested? |
| Capacity Management | Has the application been built and tested to ensure that it meets the capacity requirements? Has the capacity information provided by the application been tested and verified? Are stress and volume characteristics built into the application? |
| Availability Management | How has the application been built to address the availability requirements of the application, and how has this been tested? What testing has been done to ensure that the application meets the backup and recovery capabilities of the organisation? What happens when the application is under stress? |
| Service Continuity Management | Has the application been built to support the business recovery process following a disaster, and how has this been tested? |

| Service Level Management | Does the application meet the SLA requirements of the organisation, and has this been tested? |
| --- | --- |
| Financial Management | Has the application been built to deliver financial information, and how is this being tested? |

### 5.4.6    Organisation of the build team

The build team, like the design team, requires representation from a number of the key Service Management areas. The roles include those described in previous sections for the requirements team and the design team. These roles (discussed in detail below) are needed to ensure that Application Management and Operations are fully involved in the process of building and testing the application.

> **Tip**
>
> **By including all the key roles in testing the application, the build team will be validating all the components that affect the performance of the application once it has gone live, these being people, process, and technology. Good practice here is that no application can be signed off as having its build phase completed without the involvement and approval of all of the described roles.**

#### Change and Configuration Management (CCM)

The Change and Configuration Management role advises the developers on how to build the hooks and facilities into an application so that it conforms to the required Change and Configuration Management standards in use. This would include component identification, Change Control and status reporting, version control, software distribution, licence tracking, usage monitoring, and retirement information. The CCM role is also involved in advising how to test compliance with all of the above.

#### Support

The main involvement of the support role is working with the testers to ensure that they are able to support the application once it has gone live. An ideal activity would be for the test team to use members from the support role to maintain the application while it is in the test environment. They can then feed back any relevant experiences directly to the developers so that supportability can be fully addressed prior to the application going live.

The Service Desk could potentially be involved in User acceptance testing. This has the advantage that End Users can report Incidents through the usual channels. Service Desk staff can gain familiarity with the new application before it goes live. Problems are captured in the Information Technology Service Management (ITSM) support tool. Experienced diagnosticians will handle Incidents efficiently, whereas development staff are not always good at diagnosis.

### Operations

The operations role is similar to the support role. A member of the Operations team should actively participate in the test of the application. Ideally, the operator following the process and procedures that would be used in the live environment should run the application in a test environment.

### Security

The security role plays a major part throughout the build phase. The security role should work with the developer to ensure that the application is built to conform to organisational security standards. The role should also be involved in many other activities during this phase, but at a minimum it should assist with the following activities:

- Risk assessment of the application
- review of code and documentation
- contribution to the test plan for security compliance
- advice about trade-off decisions that affect security.

### ICT infrastructure management

The ICT infrastructure management role should help the development and testing teams to build capacity and availability management capabilities into the application so that the application will work in a predictable manner once deployed. The role should also help the development team build against the SLA that was defined in the requirements phase. Each of these areas should then be included within the testing environment to prove that the SLA realistic and provide feedback to the business if there are any issues identified with the SLA.

## 5.5    Deploy

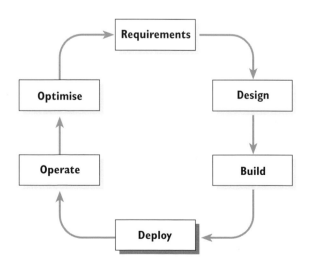

### 5.5.1    Overview

Once an application has been built, work then moves on to planning how it will be deployed within an organisation. It has long been established in the Service Management industry that most problems and issues occur as a result of change; therefore deployment needs sufficient thought and careful planning to ensure that it does not cause a problem.

The deployment phase covers the following topics:

- planning the deployment
- approving a deployment
- distributing applications
- pilot roll-outs
- management checklist for the deployment phase
- organisation of the deployment team roles.

### 5.5.2    Planning the deployment

Well planned and implemented deployment will make a significant difference to an organisation's TCO. A poorly designed deployment will, at best, force IT personnel to spend significant amounts of time troubleshooting problems and managing complexity. At worst, it can cripple the environment.

In planning a deployment, the best approach is to derive a sound set of guidelines for deployment that can be scaled from small organisations to large multinationals. Although smaller companies will have significantly less complex environments, the disciplines detailed here are still relevant.

To complete this initial activity, planners should be able to answer the questions included in Table 5.4.

*Table 5.4 – Questions to be answered when planning the deployment phase*

| | |
|---|---|
| What needs to be deployed? | Do you have a good understanding of the application that is being deployed? |
| | What are the components that make up the application? |
| | What are the business drivers for the deployment? |
| | Is it required to meet a critical business need? |
| Who are the Users? | Which Users and departments are affected by this deployment? |
| | Do they need any special training? |
| Where are the Users? | Are all the Users and systems local to the deployment, or are some remote, and how will this affect the logistics? |
| When does the deployment need to be completed? | Does the deployment need to be completed by a certain date and time or can it be completed by following a flexible schedule? |
| Why is the deployment happening? | Is the deployment needed to fix a problem or is it required for some new functionality that has been requested, and do the Users understand what is coming? |
| What is critical success? | How do you know that the deployment has been successful? |
| | How do you know when the deployment is finished? |

The answers to the above questions will drive decisions on how the application will be deployed within the environment and will include a variety of technical planning decisions, which are extensively covered in the ITIL *Service Support* and *Service Delivery* books.

Once the deployment team has the information it requires to conduct the deployment, it should have access to a deployment kit that contains the information needed for the approval of deployment and execution of the roll-out. The deployment kit would contain some or all of the following items:

- Deployment checklist and schedule document. This is a detailed document that describes all the activities and assigned responsibilities that must be completed to deliver the application. It is also a project plan describing each of the key dates and milestones that make up the deployment. This document can be considered the deployment road map.

- Deployment rollback document. This document details how the deployment can be backed out at every key stage. It contains key references to personnel, technical resources, and activities that would be needed to facilitate the successful rollback of the application.

- User sign-off document. This contains the acceptance criteria (document and tests) that need to be passed to ensure that the representative of the application's Users can sign off the deployment as successful.

### 5.5.3    Approving the deployment

Once all the above information is available, the next step is to work out the route map that the deployment will take and start seeking approval from those who work within the Change Management process.

A key goal of the Change Management process is to ensure that all parties affected by a given change are aware of and understand the impact of the impending change. Since most systems are heavily interrelated, any changes made in one part of a system might have profound impacts on another. Change Management attempts to identify all affected systems and processes before the change is implemented in order to mitigate or eliminate any adverse impacts.

Typically, this would result in the updating of the Request For Change (RFC) that was created earlier in the development cycle. The RFC are reviewed by the Change Advisory Board (CAB), which is a cross-functional group set up to evaluate change requests for business need, priority, cost/benefit, and potential impacts to other systems or processes. Typically, the CAB will make recommendations for implementation, further analysis, deferment, or cancellation.

Once approval is received for the deployment, the process of releasing the application can start.

### 5.5.4    Distributing applications

The distribution strategy is one of the Critical Success Factors for the successful deployment strategy for the application. This is a very complex topic and is comprehensively covered in the *Service Support* and *Service Delivery* books. However, for completeness, it is worth covering some of the key areas.

An application can be distributed on disks, on CDs, across networks, or over an intranet or the Internet. When the application is distributed, the following things need to be considered:

- Packaging – the application files must be packaged in such a way that one or more files can be deployed to the required locations, and a method of installing these files needs to be created. Ideally this set-up program needs to be automated, so that it will not require any human intervention.

- Deployment – at installation time, the distribution of new application executable files and support components must be clearly established. It is important to ensure that installing the new application will not affect the operation of existing applications or system components. It is also important that Users' systems can be easily upgraded to new versions when applications change, which is a matter of when, not if.

- Flexible software distribution targeting – this targeting focuses on allowing packages to be targeted at groups of Users, systems, or departments. Many systems management tools, however, provide a richer set of targeting rules. With these tools, administrators have the option to target application distribution based on hardware and software inventory properties. This allows administrators to configure and manage different levels of hardware and software on the same network.

- Deployment push functionality – the use of tools that can also schedule the time of an installation, so that client and server upgrades (and combinations of clients and servers) can be synchronised, will provide significant value to the business. Allowing applications to be pushed automatically to the right place will minimise the amount of resource needed to complete this task. Additionally, ensuring that no User logon will be required to trigger the installation means that upgrades can be deployed during off-hours.

- Pull technologies – allow a system to pull applications directly from a distribution server when they are required. This is very useful when one does not know the state or even existence of all client systems.

- Self-healing – application distribution can often go wrong for a variety of reasons such as network problems etc. Distributions that are self-healing and able to continue from a given checkpoint can save bandwidth and time.

- Patching – the size of a Release can often affect the success of a deployment, particularly when these deployments need to be run across slow network links. Providing the ability to patch a binary, rather than consuming the bandwidth necessary to send a complete file, can significantly add to the success of a Release.

- Feedback and reporting – detailed reporting, identifying the precise status of a deployment, is key to providing the personnel involved with a deployment the information that they require to maintain a high Quality of Service.

- Back-out facility – if a deployment hits unexpected problems, the systems management tools can be used to coordinate a synchronised back-out on some or all clients.

### 5.5.5    Pilot deployments

Once the deployment process has been tested successfully in the lab, there is still one important test required before the process can be used in an organisation-wide deployment – a pilot deployment.

A pilot deployment is a controlled test of the system-wide deployment, using a small subset of the production system. The pilot project does not need to be a complete test of all system functionality, but it should test enough of the system to determine whether the chosen design will work well in the production environment.

There are several good reasons for conducting pilots, among them being that they:

- document production procedures that are necessary, but are not in place in a lab environment
- determine typical and expected User interaction with the system before company-wide deployment
- help develop or modify training documentation based on pilot User feedback
- help accurately determine production environment deployment parameters
- determine the level of production support needed for the new application
- validate original functional and non-functional requirement statements.

The first pilot deployment sets the tone for the final deployment, so it is important to be completely prepared. The deliverable for this step is a swift and successful deployment process that will cause minimal or no interruption to Users. After the deployment plan has been fine-tuned with at least one pilot deployment, focusing on support materials, training, and orientation for the Users, the final deployment can start.

### Create the pilot deployment plan

The detailed pilot deployment plan will determine how and when the pilot roll-out will occur, and should provide a detailed checklist that specifies what tasks are to be done, by whom, and when.

The pilot deployment plan should be prepared for an environment complex enough for it to be similar to that of the organisation as a whole, so that the results will give the deployment team what it needs for a successful organisation-wide deployment.

### Develop pilot strategy

The pilot deployment can be used not only to test and tune the deployment plan and tools for the application, but also to evaluate End User support and training. It can also be the final deployment for early adopters.

The pilot strategy should include steps to collect feedback on the effectiveness of the deployment plan. This can include an End User survey, Service Desk call statistics, and/or End User meetings.

The pilot deployment strategy includes project definition, technical perspective, training, and support. The basic components of a complete pilot deployment strategy are described in Table 5.5.

*Table 5.5 – The components of a pilot deployment strategy*

| Pilot deployment strategy components | Decisions and issues |
|---|---|
| *Functional strategy*<br><br>Affects planning for the remaining phases of the deployment | Dependent on available time and resources<br><br>• How many pilots will be conducted, and when?<br>• How many computers will be in each pilot?<br>• Will deployments be by file server or by business function?<br>• How many simultaneous pilot deployments?<br>• Who will control the pilot deployment priorities?<br>• In what order will User deployments be conducted? |
| *Training strategy*<br><br>Affects the overall deployment strategy, plan, and schedule | How will Users be trained?<br><br>• Classroom training?<br>• Number of Users trained per week?<br>• What alternative training methods? |
| *Support strategy*<br><br>Design and implementation of support strategy must coincide with the deployment | How will the new environment be supported?<br><br>• Does the existing support model need to be modified for new application?<br>• Does the support staff need training? |

## 5.5.6 Deployment management checklist

The deployment of the application should be built and tested against the high-level manageability requirements for the organisation and any special management requirements that have been identified for the application. The deployment process needs to consider all the main ITIL Service Management functions and review how the deployment supports these. Table 5.6 provides examples of manageability checks for the deployment phase.

*Table 5.6 – Manageability checklist for the deployment phase*

| Service Management functions | Examples of deployment phase manageability checks |
|---|---|
| Configuration Management | Does the application deployment update the CMDB at each stage of the roll-out?<br>Is the deployment team using an updated inventory to complete the plan and the deployment? |
| Change Management | Is the application being deployed using the corporate Change Management process and standards? |
| Release Management | Is the application being released in a manner that minimises risks, such as a phased deployment?<br>Has a rollback option been included in the Release process for this application? |
| Security Management | Can the application be deployed in a manner that meets organisational security standards and requirements? |

| Service Management functions | Examples of deployment phase manageability checks |
|---|---|
| Incident Management | Does the deployment use the Incident Management system for reporting issues and problems?<br>Do the members of the deployment team have access to the Incident Management system so that they can record Incidents and also view Incidents that relate to the deployment? |
| Problem Management | Has a problem manager been appointed for this deployment and does the deployment team know who it is? |
| Capacity Management | Is capacity management involved in the deployment process so that it can monitor the capacity of the resources involved in the deployment? |
| Availability Management | Is availability management monitoring the availability of both the application being deployed and the rest of the IT Infrastructure to ensure that the deployment is not affecting availability?<br>How is the application's ability to be backed up and recovered during deployment being dealt with? |
| Service Continuity Management | Will any changes be required to the business recovery process following a disaster if one should occur during or after the deployment of this application? |
| Service Level Management | Is Service Level Management aware of the deployment of this application?<br>Does this application have an SLA for the deployment phase?<br>Does the application affect the SLA requirements of the organisation during deployments? |
| Financial Management | Is management accounting being done during the deployment so that the total cost of deployment can be included within the cost of ownership? |

### 5.5.7    Organisation of the deployment team

Like the other teams, the deployment team should have representation from a number of the key Service Management areas to ensure that it completes its activities comprehensively. These roles (described below) are needed to ensure that Application Management and Operations are fully involved in the entire process of deploying the application.

Change and Configuration Management (CCM)

The Change and Configuration Management role is the primary role involved with the deployment phase of an application. As previously documented, this role is responsible for

Change, Release, and Configuration Management, which are the main processes involved in moving the application from the development environment into live production use. The CCM role will use the CMBD to advise the deployment team on which Users, groups, or servers this application should be deployed to, and will provide detailed information for the planning process. The role will also assist in getting approval for the change through the Change Management process, as well as provide advice on how the application should be deployed, such as whether it should be phased or 'big bang'. The role will also advise how to use the Configuration Management system to provide tracking reports to monitor the deployment.

## Support

The support role will have significant input into planning the deployment; the work at this stage is to ensure that the correct level of resources is available to assist with supporting any Incidents that occur during the preparation and execution of the deployment. The support role is also responsible for ensuring that the Incident and Problem Management processes are able to deal with the deployment of this application.

## Operations

Similar to the support role, the operations role is also actively involved in the planning of the deployment to ensure that operations are prepared for the application from the point that it is deployed. The moment the application moves into the live environment, the operations role needs to be performing the day-to-day maintenance and operational tasks to keep the application correctly performing. While it may be several weeks or months before all Users have had the application deployed to them, a single live use of the application requires that operations treat the application like all other live applications.

## Security

The security role involvement throughout the deployment phase ensures that the application is deployed so that it does not undermine any of the organisation's security standards. The security role will be particularly interested in the planning of the deployment and will be looking for evidence of how the deployment team is ensuring that any authorised application can be deployed while keeping malicious code out of the live environment.

## ICT infrastructure management

The ICT infrastructure management role is planning and monitoring capacity and availability within the environment as the application is deployed. This role is trying to provide the deployment team with information that will make the deployment of the application predictable. It provides assessments of how the application is meeting its initial SLA, as well as advice on changes that may be needed for either the SLA or the application.

## 5.6    Operate

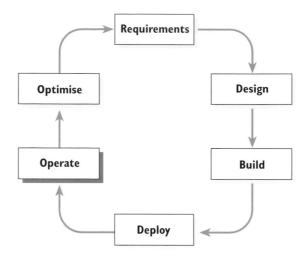

### 5.6.1    Overview

One area that is often overlooked by some application developers is what they can do to ensure that an application can be successfully operated. Recent figures from the Gartner Group show that 40% of all failures are a direct result of operations errors and a further 40% relate to applications failures (see Section 1.2).

Anything developers can do to minimise these operational failures will both improve the general availability of the application and reduce overall TCO.

Work done by a number of organisations has clearly identified that the lack of corrective maintenance cycles is directly related to the number of incidents and problems that an IT organisation will experience when an application is in operational use. Failure to perform a simple task, such as monitoring the available disk space on a server, could result in the server running out of room and causing the application to fail.

A number of key activities can be conducted during the operations phase of the lifecycle that will greatly enhance the experience of both the Operations staff and the Users.

An SLA outlines in written form the Customer's expectations of service from the Service Provider. The SLA is a method of defining responses to various service-related conditions. A typical SLA might guarantee an application that a retailer's stock control system would be available 99.5% of the time. This allows for just 50 minutes of unplanned downtime in any given week. The SLA might specify that, should this amount of unplanned downtime be exceeded, the application provider will refund the service fee for that service for that week. To facilitate such an agreement, it is important to be able to measure the performance of the application against the SLA. Normally that would require special tools that both document the expected Service Level and then provide facilities that measure the application's compliance.

Ongoing measurement of the application's performance during its operation will provide invaluable data regarding stability and bug rate, and provide management with feedback on overall quality.

Part of the measurements taken will focus on User satisfaction. How the application meets User expectation needs to be quantified to a level of detail that can be measured and reported. An example of this could include the end-to-end performance of how fast a User can connect to the application over the Internet.

Conducting a survey of Users' experiences, or creating a focus group to better understand if any areas of Users' needs are not being addressed, are also effective ways of measuring User satisfaction.

The operational process described in this section is essentially the same process as described in the *ICT Infrastructure Management* book. However, this section focuses primarily on operating applications, whereas the Operations process in *ICT Infrastructure Management* focuses on operating the ICT Infrastructure in a more general sense, although applications are part of it.

### 5.6.2    Day-to-day maintenance activities to maintain Service Levels

In well-managed environments there are relatively few 'server down' Incidents, mostly because such organisations believe in the principle of preventative maintenance and the avoidance of costly downtime. Of course, errors occur even in the best-maintained environments. Equipment fails, software develops problems, key employees leave – but in the managed environment, business continues to function. This is usually facilitated by performing day-to-day operational tasks that pre-empt problems within the applications.

Each application will have a number of tasks performed on it to ensure that is remains healthy. These tasks can be broken down into daily, weekly, monthly, and ad hoc tasks. The operational team needs to develop a profile of the application listing the tasks that need to be performed, who is responsible for performing them, and when they need to complete them.

Table 5.7 provides an example for an application.

*Table 5.7 – Example of maintenance tasks for an application*

| Daily | Check staffing level |
|---|---|
| | Review daily problem reports |
| | Review emergency change requests |
| | Execute database consistency checkers |
| | Check database server error logs |
| | Monitor network for performance or error related conditions |
| | Monitor client status |
| | Monitor server components and service status |
| | Monitor event logs on key servers |
| | Monitor system performance |
| | Monitor system directories |
| | Make a secure backup of each Systems Management Server site |
| Weekly | Attend Change Management review board |
| | Run team meetings |
| | Meet with business managers |
| | Improve database performance |
| | Check system directories |
| | Produce management reports |
| | Manage file system |

| Monthly | Compile a monthly status report |
|---|---|
| | Complete 1:1 with team members |
| | Review system health and performance |
| | Improve system performance |
| | Secure system accounts |
| | Review access to server functions |
| | Confirm site recovery from backup media |
| Ad hoc | Brainstorm with team |
| | Complete feedback survey |
| | Troubleshoot and fix problems reported |
| | Review how to make improvements to process |
| | Review status messages for security violations |
| | Amend access to security functions |

### 5.6.3    Application state

It is important to understand and practise how to restore application state. This may be needed as the result of an unplanned activity, such as hardware or system failure, or following a planned activity, such as moving or maintaining a server.

Application state is made up of several components:

- the application itself
- server-specific configuration information
- log files
- system data files
- User-specific configuration information
- User data
- network connection.

Only by understanding which of the above components makes up the application, and in what order they need to be backed up and then restored, can one successfully re-establish an application, including its application state.

The ITIL *Service Support* book defines a Configuration baseline as:

> … the configuration of a product or system established at a specific point in time, which captures both the structure and details of a configuration. It serves as reference for further activities. An application or software baseline provides the ability to change or to rebuild a specific version at a later date.

**Tip**

**Restoring application state should be tested on an ongoing and regular basis, ideally once every time the version of the application changes and more often if this occurs less than once every six months.**

### 5.6.4 Benefits of an application

An assessment of the benefits provided by the application compared with those that it was designed to deliver should be conducted in the operational phase. This assessment needs to be conducted from several viewpoints, including:

- Does the User's perception of the benefits meet those that were identified in the original requirements?
- Is the Service Level that the application delivers meeting the documented SLA?
- Is the cost of running the application in line with the forecasts originally made?
- Is the application delivering the benefits proposed in the original business case?

For the Operations team to deliver on the above, it will need management reporting combined with User surveys.

The Service Desk team working with the Operations team should identify User groups on which to conduct the periodic surveys. This information should be supplied to the application development group and IT senior management so that they can assess how Users perceive the Quality of Service that they are receiving.

Management reporting and monitoring will provide the detailed technical information that will establish whether the application is meeting its SLA. The reports will detail when the application failed to meet the SLA and why. While this could be an availability issue caused by hardware or network problems, as mentioned earlier, research shows that 80% of problems are related to application or operations issues. Therefore, it is more likely that any problems will be related to an application design issue, such as an application's inability to meet the capacity needs of a business at peak usage (a start or end of trading period, for example). The information provided by the management reports can be incorporated into improvements in the application that will help achieve an improved Service Level.

An example management report could include:

- number and type of Incidents per version of an application
- a list of problems sorted in order of priority
- a list of Users suffering the most Incidents
- a list of operational errors needing new procedures or solutions.

### 5.6.5 Operations management checklist

Operating the application will also follow a process that allows it to be run against the high-level manageability requirements for the organisation and any special management requirements that have been identified for the application. The application operability needs to consider all the main ITIL Service Management functions. Table 5.8 provides examples of manageability checks for the operating phase.

*Table 5.8 – Management checklist for the operating phase*

| Service Management functions | Examples of operating phase manageability checks |
|---|---|
| Configuration Management | Can the Operations team gain access to the Configuration Management Database so that they can confirm the application they are managing is the correct version and configured correctly? Are the operating instructions under version controls similar to those used for the application builds? |
| Change Management | Is the Operations team involved in the Change Management process; is it part of the sign-off and verification process? Does a member of the Operations team attend the Change Management meetings? |
| Release Management | Does the Release Management process ensure that deployment information is available to the operational group? Does the Operations team have access to Release information even before the application is deployed into the live environment? |
| Security Management | Does the application support the ongoing and periodic checks that Security Management needs to complete while the application is in operational use? |
| Incident Management | Does the Operations team have access to the Incident Management system and can it update information within this system? Does the Operations team understand its responsibilities in dealing with Incidents? Is the Operations team provided with reports on how well it deals with Incidents, and does it act on these? |
| Problem Management | Does the Operations team contribute to the Problem Management process, ideally by assisting with and facilitating root cause analysis? Does the Operations team meet with Problem Management on a regular basis? Does the Operations team see the weekly/monthly Problem Management report? |
| Capacity Management | Is capacity management information being monitored and reported on as this application is run, and is this information provided to Capacity Management? |
| Availability Management | How is the application's availability being measured, and is this information being fed back to the Availability Management function within the IT organisation? |
| Service Continuity Management | Is the business recovery process for the application tested regularly by Operations? |

| Service Level Management | Is the SLA visible and understood by the Operations team so that it appreciates how its running of the application affects the delivery of the SLA? Does Operations see the weekly/monthly SLA report? |
| --- | --- |
| Financial Management | Does Operations provide input into the financial information about the application? For example, if an application requires an operator to perform additional tasks at night, is this recorded? |

### 5.6.6    Organisation of the Operations team

The Operations team, like the other teams, will require representation from a number of the key Service Management areas. These roles (described below) are needed to ensure that Application Management and Operations are fully involved in the process of running and operating the application in the live IT environment.

### Change and Configuration Management (CCM)

The Change and Configuration Management role advises and works with Operations on such issues as ensuring that the application running in the live environment is the right version and that it is still correctly configured. The role also ensures that the operating instructions that the operators use are up to date. This role is also responsible for information about potential changes to the live environment, as well as identifying and discussing any potential issues that might come about as a result of this change. The CCM role should ensure that the operations role is fully involved in the Release of a new version and signs off and resources each of these. If the Release needs to be rolled back, the CCM should ensure that the operations role is fully aware of this and knows which version to operate.

### Support

The support role works closely with the Operations team addressing any Incidents that might materialise during use. The role is also responsible for informing operations of any Incidents that will affect, or are affecting, the work of operations. Getting operations working again should be a key concern of the support role.

### Operations

The operations role is the main role involved in this phase. It manages the daily operations, database and system administration activities to run and maintain the application and IT services. The operations role performs the scheduled and repeatable processes, such as data backup, archiving and storage, output management, system monitoring and event log management, and print and file server management. The operations role is ultimately accountable for the application being run correctly against agreed operational procedures.

### Security

The security role will focus on ensuring that the application is operated in a manner that does not undermine any of the organisation's security standards. This role will also undertake periodic and sometimes spot audits of operational security procedures and practice. This role will also audit security log files to ensure compliance with working practices.

### ICT infrastructure management

During the operating phase, the infrastructure management role is mainly concerned with working with the operations role to gather capacity and availability management information. The role also provides strong third-line technical support when incidents require additional help, and would normally work with the operations and support roles in delivering this. The infrastructure management role is interested in gathering operational metrics during this phase that will help plan improvements in the optimising phase.

## 5.7    Optimise

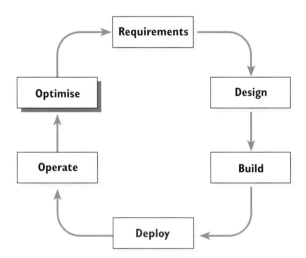

### 5.7.1    Overview

All applications that have been in live production use for a period of time need to have this use periodically reviewed against a set of criteria that assesses whether the application should continue to be used 'as is' or whether it requires modification or retirement.

This section covers the following topics:

- application review process
    - no change
    - modification or change required
    - application retirement
- management checklist for the optimise phase
- organisation of the optimisation team roles.

### 5.7.2    Application review process

The use and performance of each application should be reviewed periodically to ascertain whether the application is continuing to meet the ongoing needs of the business or the technical requirements of the infrastructure that it is operating within. The review process can be initiated by a number of conditions, for instance:

- a fixed period of time has passed since the last review (for example, 12–24 months)
- Problem Management has identified issues with the current version that require modifications
- business requirements are changing and the use of the current application needs to be reviewed against these new requirements
- the technical infrastructure that the application relies on has changed and the application needs to be reviewed against this.

The review process should assess the application against a number of areas, such as people, business process, and technology, and also will need to confirm answers to some of the questions given in Table 5.9.

*Table 5.9 – Questions for the application review process*

| Areas | Questions |
|---|---|
| People | Are the needs of the Users being addressed by the application, and, if not, which areas require change or improvement? |
| | Is use of the application intuitive so that it does not require an unreasonable level of training to use? |
| | Are Users making an unreasonably large number of mistakes while using this system compared with other similar applications? |
| Business process | Has the mission of the application owner changed, and, if so, how does the application meet this new mission? |
| | Will a change in organisational structure affect the use or functional needs of this application? |
| | Will an external change, such as new legislation, affect the application? |
| | Have the Service Level requirements changed? |
| Technology | Does the application fail to meet its Service Level due to technical issues? If so, what are these technical issues? |
| | Are there any technical improvements or changes that will necessitate a change to the application? If so, how will it need to change? |
| | How has the application performed in operational use and what improvements and changes will affect this? |
| | What is the application's performance against SLA targets? |
| | What are the operational and manageability aspects and performance against operational targets? |
| | How do support processes and performance comply with OLA targets and contractual targets? |

As mentioned in Chapter 3, the application portfolio could, if used, provide many of the answers to the questions listed above.

By answering these questions, the application review process will categorise the change as one of the following:

- no changes required
- a change is required in the application and an RFC should be prepared
- retire application as it is no longer required.

A good practice is to give the optimisation team access to an application staging environment so that it can verify that the improvement will not itself cause any other issues. All too often organisations dismantle their test and staging environments after deployment and leave the optimisation team with inadequate facilities.

### No change required

Unless they are being used in a very dynamic environment, the majority of applications will not require any changes, and the only action needed is to record the details of the review in the application portfolio and set a date for the next review.

### Modification or change required

If a change is required in the application assessment, a proposal should be prepared. It will detail what changes are required in the application, and should include:

- the change required
- business need and business justification
- who is responsible for the change
- the amount of effort needed to complete the change
- the prerequisites for the change
- when the change needs to be completed
- who the stakeholders are
- the success criterion for the change.

Depending on the type of change, the Users might have significant involvement in the optimisation phase providing details of new business requirements.

A good practice is to give the optimisation team access to the application test environment so that it can verify that the improvement will not itself cause any other issues. All too often organisations dismantle their test environments after deployment and leave the optimisation team with inadequate facilities.

The modification proposal is then used to drive a new iteration through the application lifecycle, including the starting of a new development process. It also would result in the creation of an RFC in the Change Management system.

### Application retirement

When an application is identified as no longer being required, the assessment would generate a retirement proposal. This proposal should provide a road map of how the application will be removed from live service. If the application is sufficiently complex, it might require the creation of tools or code from the development team to facilitate its retirement. Change Management should also be involved in the retirement process, since the retirement will result in a change to the environment. All application components, such as executables, configuration files, source code, log files, and references to the application, should be removed.

Complex retirement projects might also require the creation of special applications to facilitate the removal of the original application from live use. This new special application should also follow the application lifecycle. This issue arises regularly in reviewing outdated legacy applications. Retirement of an application may require changes to the SLAs if business functions or applications are specifically mentioned. The planning for this needs to ensure that this happens. There may be legal or other requirements that require retired applications to be archived, for example, to allow retrieval of archived data.

### 5.7.3 Optimisation management checklist

The optimisation process should consider all the main ITIL Service Management functions and review how this phase supports them. Table 5.10 provides examples of manageability checks for the optimising phase.

*Table 5.10 – Management checklist for the optimising phase*

| *Service Management functions* | *Examples of optimise phase manageability checks* |
| --- | --- |
| Configuration Management | As the application is reviewed within the optimise phase, is the CMDB used to assist with the review? Are Configuration Management personnel involved in the optimisation process, including providing advice in the use of and updating the inventory? |
| Change Management | As modifications are identified within this phase, does the team use the Change Management system to coordinate the changes? Does the optimisation team understand the Change Management process? |
| Release Management | Do members of the optimisation team understand the Release process, and are they using this for planning the deployment of the optimisation to the environment? Is Release Management involved in providing advice to the assessment process? |
| Incident Management | Do members of the optimisation team have access to the Incident Management system so that they can record Incidents and also view Incidents that may be addressed in optimisation? |
| Problem Management | Is the optimisation process being provided with information by Problem Management to incorporate into the assessment process? |
| Capacity Management | Is capacity management feeding information into the optimisation process? |
| Availability Management | Does the assessment use the availability information to complete the proposal of modifications that are needed to the application? Is any improvement required in the application's ability to be backed up and recovered? |
| Service Continuity Management | What optimisation is required in the business recovery process to meet the business needs? |

| Service Management functions | Examples of optimise phase manageability checks |
|---|---|
| Service Level Management | Is Service Level Management information available for inclusion in the optimisation process? |
| Financial Management | Is financial information available to be included in the assessment process? |

### 5.7.4 Organisation of the optimisation team

As with all the other teams, the optimisation team will require the involvement from a number of the key Service Management areas to ensure that the activities of the phase are completed comprehensively, and that Application Management and Operations are fully involved in assessing and optimising an application. The roles are described below.

#### Change and Configuration Management (CCM)

The Change and Configuration Management role provides the optimisation team members with the configuration information that they need to perform the assessment. The role also provides information regarding the Change Management process, Release information, and information from the configuration database that can help with the assessment. The CCM role is also involved in taking the output from the assessment and ensuring that those involved in the Change Management process are aware of the required changes and fully involved.

#### Support

The support role will provide input into the optimisation phase ensuring that issues and problems that have been experienced in live usage are included and addressed in the assessment. The support role also provides support and assistance to the optimisation team members with any issues that they may experience during optimisation.

#### Operations

The operations role is involved in the assessment by identifying any operational weaknesses in running the application in live usage. Many issues that affect reliability of an application can relate to how easy or intuitive it is to operate, which makes this information valuable. Also, information relating to how the regular (daily, weekly, monthly etc.) tasks integrate with the rest of the operations workload can affect the efficiency and reliability of the application, and this needs to be assessed.

#### Security

The security role provides input into how the application can be optimised into being more secure or to have greater levels of integrity as far as business/User data and enhancing the protection of other corporate assets are concerned. The security role is also particularly interested in the planning that goes on in this phase to ensure that any changes or improvements that may be proposed comply with the corporate security standards.

## ICT infrastructure management

The ICT infrastructure management role normally would take a leading role through the optimisation phase, providing technical expertise on a number of technical and Service Management disciplines including:

- advice on capacity management issues and how to circumvent them
- information on how to design greater availability into the application
- advice on which technology and tools should be considered to help optimise the application.

The ICT infrastructure management role is usually best placed to lead this phase, as those in it have an understanding of the application. They also have experience from working across the application portfolio, together with the technical skills and the vision needed to advise a development team on improvements that can be made to the application.

## 6 ORGANISING ROLES AND FUNCTION

### 6.1 Team dynamics

At the heart of effective Application Management is an effective team. Teams that work effectively produce quality applications. The opposite of this is also true. Gartner Group research indicates that 40% of the problems encountered during the operate phase of an application's lifecycle are caused by programming errors. Some of these might be individual programmer errors that would have occurred no matter how effective the application team was. But many of them are team-based errors that occur because of misinterpretation of standards or because of a lack of communication during the development process. The following example demonstrates the effect of such miscommunication.

**Example**

Two companies agreed to develop a service for the Customers of both companies. This new service would enable the Customers to conduct transactions concerning the companies' products and services more easily. In order to build this service, each company needed to develop new applications and update existing ones. The new applications had to communicate with each other through a specified communications protocol. However, one of the companies did not have the experience and skills on this specific communications protocol and was therefore not able to translate the specification into a working system. The result was that the project exceeded the budget by twofold and the service eventually delivered to the Customers of both companies did not meet the intended Service Levels.

So what are the things that have a positive effect on the way that a team performs? Here are some of the most important:

- having a shared project vision
- working as a team of peers
- understanding the business
- having overlapping roles and shared responsibilities
- using tension metrics.

#### 6.1.1 Shared project vision

Fundamental to the success of a project is that team members and the Customer have a shared project vision. That means they have a clear, shared understanding of the goals and objectives for the project. This may be different depending on whether it is at a single application level or at the application portfolio level. Team members and Customers all bring with them assumptions about what the project is going to do for the organisation. Creating a shared vision brings those assumptions to light and ensures that all project participants are working to accomplish the same set of goals.

Without a shared vision, team members will have competing views, generally resulting in communication problems. Delivering results as a cohesive group will be difficult and, if the team does deliver, members will have difficulty determining their success because it will depend on which vision they measure it by.

### 6.1.2    Team of peers

The team-of-peers concept places equal value on each role in a team. This enables unrestricted communication between the roles, increases team accountability, and reinforces the concept that the goals of each role are equally important and all must be achieved. To be successful with the team of peers, all roles must have ownership of the requirements that must be met, must act as Customer advocates, and must understand what business problem they are trying to solve.

While each role has an equal value on the team, there are differences between roles within the team. Placing equal value on each role should not be confused with consensus-driven decision-making. Each role has its purpose and goals and must therefore be mandated to achieve its goals. This means that a team of peers will have some form of hierarchy for the purposes of distributing work and managing resources.

### 6.1.3    Understanding the business

It is not enough for a team to be technically competent in software development in order to be successful. Many a 'great' product did not meet the business objectives of the Customer and, though well designed and technically sound, was shelved. To prevent this, team members need a clear understanding of the business problem that they are trying to solve.

One way to accomplish this is to have active Customer participation and feedback throughout the development process. This includes Customer participation in establishing the product vision, signing off what is going to be built, establishing and agreeing to a schedule, taking part in trade-off decisions, and adding feedback through usability studies and test beta releases.

Another method is to continually ensure that every requirement in the product design, functional and non-functional, can be traced back to the key business drivers outlined by the Customer. If a feature cannot be traced back, then the team should question whether to spend development time on this activity. An ideal approach is to link this activity back to the Change Management process and ensure that requirements are formally accepted or rejected.

### 6.1.4    Overlapping roles and shared responsibilities

As Chris Peters humorously put it in a 1991 presentation:

> **'It's extremely important to move responsibility very low in the organisation. Your goal is not to be working on a project where you can't sleep at night. Your goal isn't to have it so that the project leads can't sleep at night. Your goal is so that nobody sleeps at night. And when nobody is sleeping at night, you have pushed responsibility to the proper level.'**

To encourage team members to work closely with each other, give them broad, interdependent, and overlapping roles, so that they all share responsibility for shipping the right product at the right time. This approach discourages the sort of specialisation among team members that often leads to isolated, rather than collaborative, effort.

### 6.1.5    Tension metrics

As discussed in Chapter 4, each team effort is a balance of resources (people and money), features (the product or service and its quality), and the schedule. The delivered product or service therefore represents a balanced trade-off between these three elements. Tension metrics can help create that balance by preventing teams from focusing on just one element – for example, on delivering the product or service on time. If a project is being driven primarily towards satisfying a business driver of on-time delivery to the exclusion of other factors, the project manager will achieve this aim by flexing the resources and application features in order to meet the delivery schedule. This unbalanced focus will therefore either lead to budget increases or lower product quality. Tension metrics help create a delicate balance between shared goals and delivering a product or service according to business requirements within time and budget. Tension metrics do not, however, conflict with shared goals and values, but rather prevent teams from taking shortcuts and shirking on their assignment. Tension metrics can therefore be seen as a tool to create shared responsibilities between team members with different roles in the application lifecycle.

All too often project schedules slip during design and build phases due to unforeseen circumstances. One way to meet the delivery date would be to limit testing to urgent issues only, with the result that the application(s) are deployed with a questionable quality level. A team can, however, have to meet both the goal of deploying its application on time and that of shipping an application that has less than, for example, 30 bugs found within the first 30 days of production. These conflicting goals make sure that a development team has a responsibility that persists into the operate phase of the lifecycle. Establishing tense goals such as these ensures that teams will make more conscious trade-offs among the triangular relationship of resources, features, and schedule. Tension metrics are not new to project management best practices. However, most projects and project managers are inclined to focus on rather short-term goals, not exceeding the scope and lifetime of the project. This narrow focus justifies extra attention to the use of objectives for teams and individuals that have a larger span than the area of their immediate responsibility.

There is an abundance of literature on establishing teams, balancing among team roles suggested by Belbin, and creating team spirit through open communication. Although much more can be said about team dynamics and managing teams, most of these practices can be applied to teamwork outside the Application Management lifecycle. This section focuses on some aspects of team dynamics of specific interest to the Application Management lifecycle. Team dynamics and the culture of teams and organisations are largely influenced by the goals set and measured by the organisation. The way people behave in teams and processes largely depends on how they are measured for their performance on teams and processes. The next section briefly discusses some issues concerning goals and metrics.

## 6.2    Goals and metrics

Each phase of the application lifecycle requires very specific contributions from the key roles identified in Chapter 5, each of which has very specific goals to meet. Ultimately, the quality of the application will be determined by how well each role meets its goals, and by how well those sometimes conflicting goals are managed along the way. That makes it crucial that organisations find some way of measuring performance – by applying a set of metrics to each goal.

### 6.2.1  Breaking down goals and metrics

It is really outside the scope of this book to dig too deeply into human resources management, and besides, there is no shortage of literature already available on the subject. However, there are some specific things that can be said about best practices for goals and metrics as they apply to managing applications in their lifecycle.

Many IT service organisations measure their IT professionals on an abstract and high-level basis. During appraisal and counselling, most managers discuss such things as 'taking part in one or more projects/performing activities of a certain kind', or 'fulfilling certain roles in projects/ activities' and 'following certain courses'. Although accomplishing such goals might be important for the professional growth of an individual, it does not facilitate the application lifecycle or any specific process in it. In reality, most IT service organisations do not use more detailed performance measures that are in line with key business drivers, because it is difficult to do, and do correctly.

But there is a way. In previous chapters, key business drivers were translated into Service Level requirements (SLRs) and operations level requirements. The latter consisted of process, skills, and technology requirements. What that constituted, really, was a translation from a business requirement into requirements for IT services and IT components. There is also the question, discussed in Section 3.1, of the strategic position of IT. In essence, the question is whether IT is an enabler or a cost centre, the answer to which determines the requirements for the IT services and IT components. The answer also determines how the processes in the application lifecycle are executed, and how the people in the organisation should behave. If IT is a cost centre, applications might be developed to run mostly on central systems in order to reduce Total Cost of Ownership (TCO). Applications will have those characteristics that will reduce total costs of ownership throughout the lifecycle. On the other hand, if IT is an enabler, applications will be designed to flexibly adjust to changing business requirements and meet early time-to-market objectives.

Either way, the important point is that those requirements for IT services and IT components would determine how processes in the lifecycle are measured and managed, and thus how the performance and growth of professionals should be measured.

Best practice shows that goals and metrics can be classified into three categories: financial metrics, learning and growth metrics, and organisational or process effectiveness metrics. An example of financial metrics might be the expenses and total percentage of hours spent on projects or maintenance, while an example of learning and growth might be the percentage of education pursued in a target skill area, certification in a professional area, and contribution to Knowledge Management. These metrics will not be discussed in this book.

The last type of metrics, organisational or process effectiveness metrics, can be further broken down into product quality metrics and process quality metrics. Product quality metrics are the metrics supporting the contribution to the delivery of quality products. Examples of product quality metrics are shown in Table 6.1. Process quality metrics are the quality metrics related to efficient and effective process management. Examples of process quality metrics are shown in Table 6.2.

*Table 6.1 – Examples of product quality metrics*

| Measure | Metric | Quality goal | Lower limit | Upper limit |
|---|---|---|---|---|
| Size | % variation of software product against initial estimate | Within 20% of estimate | Not to be less than 20% of estimate | Not to exceed 20% of estimate |
| Schedule | % variation against revised plan | Within 7.5% of estimate | Not to be less than 7.5% of estimate | Not to exceed 7.5% of estimate |
| Effort | % variation against revised plan | Within 10% of estimate | Not to be less than 10% of estimate | Not to exceed 10% of estimate |
| Cost | % variation against revised plan | Within 10% of estimate | Not to be less than 10% of estimate | Not to exceed 10% of estimate |
| Defects | % variation against planned defect density | Within 10% of estimate | Not to be less than 10% of estimate | Not to exceed 10% of estimate |
| Productivity | % variation against productivity goal | Within 10% of estimate | Not to be less than 10% of estimate | Not to exceed 10% of estimate |
| Customer satisfaction | Customer satisfaction survey result | Larger than 8.9 on the range of 1 to 10 | Not to be less than 8.9 on the range of 1 to 10 | |

*Table 6.2 – Examples of process quality metrics*

| Measure | Metric | Quality goal | |
|---|---|---|---|
| Productivity | Average development productivity | 0.19 function points per hour | 26.6 function points per month |
| | Development productivity per language | | |
| | Development productivity per platform | | |
| Review | Document pages | 8 hours per page | |
| | Test case execution | 1 hour per case | |
| | Software quality assurance (SQA) | 16 hours per review | |
| Defects | Defect removal efficiency | >95% | |
| | Delivered defects | <0.025 per function point | |

## 6.2.2    Using organisational metrics

To be effective, measurements and metrics should be woven through the complete organisation, touching the strategic as well as the tactical level. To successfully support the key business drivers, the IT services manager needs to know what and how well each part of the organisation contributes to the final success.

It is also important, when defining measurements for goals that support the IT services strategy, to remember that measurements must focus on results and not on efforts. Focus on the organisational output and try to get clear what the contribution is. This can best be done following the processes defined in Chapter 5. Each stage in the lifecycle has its processes and contribution to the application. Each stage of the lifecycle also has its roles, which contribute to the development or management of the application. Based on the process goals and the quality attributes of the applications, goals and metrics can be defined for each role in the processes of the lifecycle. An example of roles attached to certain process steps can be seen in Figure 6.1.

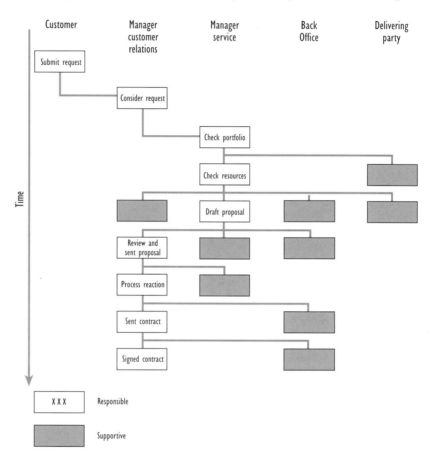

Figure 6.1 – Contributions of different roles in a process

Once the contribution of a role in a process is known, and the process goal and process output are known, goals and metrics can be assigned to a role in relation to the process goal and output. Roles are mapped on functions and thus functions get the goals and metrics that are assigned to the roles. Based on the goals and metrics assigned to the roles, an organisation can make sound judgements on combining roles into functions. Roles with conflicting goals and metrics should not be combined into functions, while roles with goals and metrics that reinforce each other can be combined into functions.

Although this designed approach should work well for designing and building an organisation, it is mostly useful in green-field situations. However, these situations are not that common. Organisations growing to a higher process maturity level are not likely to take this designer's approach. An existing organisation will analyse the roles professionals fulfil in a process and assign goals and metrics to these professionals based on process efficiency and product quality. This pragmatic approach works well and should not be less useful than the designer's approach. The drawback, however, is that possible role conflicts might not be considered.

## 6.3 Collaboration and Knowledge Management

### 6.3.1 Introduction

Knowledge Management is a rapidly growing practice that seeks to maximise the value of an organisation by helping its people to innovate, adapt, and respond to the increasing demands placed upon them. As the world economy continues to shift from a pure production-based value system to an intellectual- and skills-based one, Knowledge Management is rapidly becoming a key competitive advantage in virtually all industries. This phenomenon has put the IT Service Provider in a relatively unique position. Not only must IT provide the platform and tool sets for the modern knowledge worker, the IT group must utilise this same Knowledge Management infrastructure in order to successfully, and competitively, provide services. Collaborating and managing information across all phases of the application lifecycle is not only best practice but a requirement for survival in the modern IT environment. So what exactly is Knowledge Management?

Knowledge Management is first and foremost a management discipline that treats intellectual capital as a managed asset. This includes the capture and flow of an organisation's data, information, and knowledge, and the delivery of it to individuals and groups engaged in accomplishing specific tasks. The primary goal of Knowledge Management is to manage the intellectual capacity of the firm for the knowledge workers who make the daily decisions that ultimately determine the success or failure of a business. Knowledge Management is not about creating a central database that is a complete replica of all that is known by employees, or that is embedded in the systems they use. On the contrary, Knowledge Management is about embracing a diversity of knowledge sources, from databases, websites, employees, and partners, and, in turn, cultivating that knowledge where it resides, while capturing its context and giving it greater meaning by utilising it for the benefit of other parts of the company. The essence of Knowledge Management involves fuelling what knowledge workers do best, what Microsoft CEO Bill Gates refers to as 'thinking work'.

Knowledge Management is a very broad subject area and one which itself deserves much more attention than would be appropriate to provide in a book about Application Management. For this reason, this section is limited to a description of Knowledge Management fundamentals and an overview of the basic knowledge services that would form the foundation of a solid Knowledge Management solution. This section concludes with a description of things to consider when applying these Knowledge Management services to Application Management.

### 6.3.2 Knowledge Management fundamentals

Knowledge has its roots in three primary areas, all of which must be considered when developing a Knowledge Management solution. People gain knowledge from their experiences and their peers' expertise, as well as from the analysis of data such as sales figures, financial reports, production statistics, and system metrics. Through the synthesis of these three elements, new knowledge is created and opportunities are shaped. Effective Knowledge Management strategies manage and foster all these sources of new knowledge:

1   **Data** is generally characterised as a set of discrete facts about events in and around business activities. Most organisations capture significant amounts of data in highly structured databases such as Customer Relations Management (CRM) systems, data warehouses, ERP, and Manufacturing Resource Planning (MRP) line-of-business applications. In addition, most firms subscribe to external data sources that provide demographic data, competitive statistics, and other market intelligence. The key Knowledge Management activity around this data is in the ability to analyse, synthesise, and then transform the data into information and knowledge.

2   **Information** is the outcome of capturing and providing context to experiences and ideas. Information (or explicit experiences) is typically stored in semi-structured content such as documents, e-mail, voice mail and multimedia. The key Knowledge Management activity around information is managing the content in a way that makes it easy to find, reuse, and learn from experiences so that mistakes are not repeated and work is not duplicated.

3   **Knowledge** is composed of the tacit experiences, ideas, insights, values, and judgements of individuals. It is therefore 'in a person's head', and so only small parts can be transformed into information for other professionals in the organisation. It is dynamic and can be accessed only through the direct collaboration and communication with experts who have knowledge. Knowledge Management initiatives must provide the cultural incentives for sharing the personal experiences that have historically constituted an individual's value to a firm. Today, an individual's contribution to a firm is in the creation of new knowledge through the collaboration with others in synthesising existing data and information.

The above elements are all considered knowledge assets because they represent the elements that a corporation must manage in order to ensure a dynamic, innovative, and agile organisation. Without properly managing these assets, a company cannot grow effectively, information is lost, lessons are not learned, work is prolonged, tasks are repeated, trends go unnoticed, and completed jobs are repeated.

It should be noted that the above descriptions apply equally to hard-core business functions such as sales and marketing as well as all aspects of IT Service Management, including Application Management.

### 6.3.3   Knowledge services

With the increasing complexity of IT Service Delivery and subsequently of Application Management, it is becoming more difficult for IT professionals to manage all the various aspects required to deliver quality business services. There are more groups, applications, technologies, organisations, Customers, suppliers, and Users involved than at any time in the history of information technology. Many of today's business transactions can be completed successfully only if the IT services of all the parties involved perform their respective functions in a highly available and responsive manner. The obvious example of this can be found in today's modern Internet economy. The complex value chain of goods and services provided over the Internet both to consumers and businesses is the clearest evidence of this increasing complexity.

As a result, the toughest challenge for IT professionals today is to deliver business services in a seamless manner to their Customers and business partners when the execution of these services is not completely within their control. So what is the key to operating successfully in this environment? The answer is the sharing of data, information and knowledge across all groups involved, both internally and externally, in a safe and timely manner. In other words, it is using Knowledge Management discipline with respect to one's knowledge assets. This can most easily be accomplished through the implementation of knowledge services to the members of the team(s) involved. There are four general categories of knowledge services:

1  **Collaboration** is the process of sharing tacit knowledge and working together to accomplish stated goals and objectives. Everyone has collaborated in some fashion during their lives to accomplish a set of objectives that required the efforts of many people. The process of interaction and the sharing of knowledge and workload is collaboration. The following is a list of knowledge services widely available today, which, properly implemented, can significantly improve the productivity of people by streamlining and improving the way they collaborate:

    – shared calendars and tasks
    – threaded discussions
    – instant messaging
    – white-boarding
    – video or teleconferencing
    – e-mail.

2  **Content Management** is the process by which explicit experience is captured and managed. The result is often a knowledge asset represented in written words, figures, graphics, and other forms of knowledge presentation. In order for organisations to maximise the benefits of these knowledge assets, they must capture, organise, control, share, and publish the content. Examples of knowledge services which directly support content management are:

    – word processing
    – data and financial analysis
    – presentation tools
    – flow-charting
    – content management systems (codify, organise, version control, document architectures)
    – publication and distribution.

3  **Communities** are rapidly becoming the method of choice for groups of people spread across time zones and country boundaries to communicate, collaborate, and share knowledge. These communities are typically facilitated through an on-line medium such as an intranet or extranet and the community often acts as the integration point for all knowledge services provided to its members. Well-run communities will typically elect a leader to manage and run the community and a group of subject matter experts to contribute and evaluate knowledge assets within the community. Examples of services and functions provided within the typical on-line community are:

    – community portals
    – e-mail alias management
    – focus groups
    – intellectual property, best practice, work example, and template repository
    – on-line events and net shows.

Successful communities often implement a reward and recognition programme for their members. Such a programme is a means to acknowledge and reward the contribution of valuable knowledge assets. These assets are submitted by members of the community and are evaluated by the community leader and elected subject matter experts. The assets that are determined to be of high value to the community are deemed 'gems' and the author(s) are recognised within the community and meaningfully rewarded in some fashion for their contribution. This is a highly effective way to encourage members to share their knowledge and move past the old paradigm that knowledge is power and job security and therefore needs to be hoarded. In addition, it is highly recommended that senior management actively participates in these communities to foster a culture and environment that rewards knowledge sharing and collaboration.

4  **Workflow management** is another broad area of knowledge services that provides systemic support for managing knowledge assets through a pre-defined workflow or process. Many knowledge assets today go through a workflow process that creates, modifies, augments, informs, or approves aspects of the asset. For example, within the sphere of Application Management, a Request For Change (RFC) is a knowledge asset that moves through a workflow that creates it, modifies it, assesses it, estimates it, approves it, and ultimately deploys it. Workflow applications provide the infrastructure and support necessary to implement a highly efficient process to accomplish these types of tasks. Typical workflow services provided within this services category include:

   − workflow design
   − routing objects
   − event services
   − state transition services.

### 6.3.4    Knowledge Management and Application Management

Effective Knowledge Management is a powerful asset for people in all roles across all phases of the application lifecycle. It is an excellent method for individuals and teams to share data, information, and knowledge about all facets of an application or IT service. From business processes and requirements through to operations and support guidance, effective Knowledge Management is increasingly a best practice differentiator. A growing trend in today's IT industry is to deploy and manage fewer, more intelligent applications. What are needed are applications that can be modified quickly in response to business needs. In order to accomplish this, the industry is discovering that knowledge workers must incorporate their know-how and intelligence into the applications and services used to run the business in every phase of the application lifecycle. It does not do any good for a company to have the capability of building and deploying new functionality quickly, if accurate and concise business requirements cannot be determined in a similar time-frame. The same holds true in reverse. Although not the total answer, properly deployed Knowledge Management services can be a big help in achieving a balanced approach across the application lifecycle.

Since it is highly impractical to apply the same level of Knowledge Management services support throughout all phases of the application lifecycle, Table 6.3 attempts to highlight the key Knowledge Management services that most benefit participants in the respective phases of the application lifecycle. It is certainly acknowledged that most Knowledge Management services would be beneficial across every phase; this table merely highlights the most critical Knowledge Management services to consider throughout the lifecycle.

*Table 6.3 – Key Knowledge Management services for each application lifecycle phase*

| Lifecycle phase | Key Knowledge Management activities |
| --- | --- |
| Requirements | Project vision, scope and requirements definition, and approval, all require high levels of collaboration. The more dispersed the people, groups, and business functions are, the more important collaboration support becomes. Knowledge of business functions and business value of IT is also crucial to the effective capturing and managing of requirements. |
| Design | A required Knowledge Management service is to ensure a design that is responsive to requirements, collaboration and content management. Managing reference designs and earlier designs of similar projects will decrease lead times dramatically and improve quality due to earlier references. |
| Build | During the build phase, content management becomes increasingly important and requires more sophisticated techniques for managing project documents, application and systems code, as well as test plans, scripts, and guides. Management of reusable components, both built and tested, can also be seen as Knowledge Management that enhances the quality and lead time of the build phase. |
| Deploy | Again, collaboration and content management are critical Knowledge Management services during this phase. In particular, during application installation and IT service cut-over activities, the Knowledge Management services within the collaboration area are vital in order to ensure smooth deployments with little or no downtime in services provided to the Customer. Especially in distributed environments, information about the target's environments is key in order to ensure a smooth deployment. |
| Operate | Within the operations phase, collaboration and Content Management remain highly utilised services. Content Management becomes very important here and Change and Configuration Management in particular are prime examples of a sophisticated Content Management process. This phase also benefits from the Knowledge Management services around communities and workflow. There are many operations tasks that lend themselves nicely to workflow automation and the ongoing nature of operations is supported well by the establishment of a formal community. For third-line support, much knowledge will remain tacit. However, the goal of the formal communities is to make part of that knowledge explicit in order to increase first-line Incident resolution. |
| Optimise | The activities in the optimise phase continue to benefit from collaboration, but also from document management services. As disparate teams analyse IT service and application usage, performance, and support issues in order to reach a consensus on future directions, Knowledge Management services, like the communities, collaboration and document management described in this section, are valuable assets to take advantage of. |

### 6.3.5    Barriers to successful Knowledge Management solutions

There are many elements that determine the degree of success or failure that any given project will achieve, and Knowledge Management projects are certainly no different. This paragraph provides some insight into the most common barriers to successful Knowledge Management projects with a few recommendations of how to overcome them. Following these recommendations will by no means guarantee success, but the reader might find them helpful in developing unique strategies to address these barriers within their own company environment. To begin, Figure 6.2 shows the major barriers to successful Knowledge Management implementations. The following paragraphs discuss each barrier and how to avoid having it derail a Knowledge Management project.

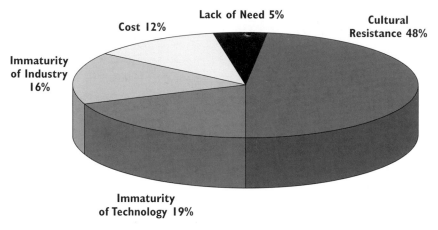

*Figure 6.2 – Barriers to Knowledge Management implementation*

### Cultural resistance

The most common barrier to projects of all kinds resides in the culture of the organisations, groups, teams, and individuals involved. Knowledge Management projects are particularly vulnerable to this phenomenon because, for advanced Knowledge Management services to work effectively, knowledge must be shared freely and willingly. This is often the exact opposite of how knowledge workers have historically been rewarded. Why? Because to get ahead in many corporate cultures, building and retaining key knowledge was a sign of intelligence, and applying that knowledge as an individual or small team was seen as being successful. Today, there is a broader need for knowledge sharing, which is both empowering and risky depending on the cultural environment established. It is for this reason that great care must be taken by the executives and project sponsors to plan activities and processes that explicitly address this issue.

A technique that has proven to be quite effective in combating cultural resistance is a well thought out reward and recognition programme. Providing meaningful and valuable rewards for stellar contributions to the corporate knowledge base is a powerful incentive. Many organisations have institutionalised this incentive by making it part of the appraisal and counselling programme. This reflects back to the goals and metrics discussion in Section 6.2 where contribution to intellectual capital was cited as one of the metrics professionals in the organisation can be measured by. Cash bonuses, stock options, travel awards, gift certificates, and additional vacation days are a few tangible and valuable examples that might be included in a rewards programme. To implement a programme that includes reward without recognition is simply a fool's quest. Generally, people appreciate genuine recognition and gratitude more than anything else in the work environment. This includes recognition from peers, management, senior executives and, as appropriate, partners and Customers. Do not underestimate the power of a well-planned rewards and recognition programme; just remember to ensure that it is genuine, long-lasting, and applied fairly.

Another key element to successful Knowledge Management projects is leadership, which, although a bit less tangible than a rewards and recognition programme, is none the less a critical ingredient. Leadership needs to send a simple, clear message that sharing and innovation fostered by Knowledge Management are important to the organisation. By funding high-profile projects, encouraging systemic innovation, and making mental agility and innovation a personal priority, management can create an atmosphere that fosters the cultural shifts necessary to get buy-in from its most valuable resource, its people.

### Immaturity of the Knowledge Management industry and technologies

The second most common barrier to successful Knowledge Management projects revolves around the IT industry's ability to deliver Knowledge Management solutions. This includes both the underlying technologies and the Knowledge Management capabilities and competency of solution providers. Although Knowledge Management has at its roots many well-established technologies and practices, there are many new innovations under way which are still in a relatively immature state. With the focus and attention placed upon intellectual property and thus Knowledge Management, this immaturity and lack of experience should soon disappear.

In the meantime, however, careful planning and a phased approach to deploying Knowledge Management services is recommended. Start with proven Knowledge Management services such as e-mail, shared calendars, and content management systems, and follow these with more sophisticated services such as workflow management and communities.

### Cost and lack of need

Finally, the remaining two barriers to Knowledge Management implementation are cost and lack of need. Obviously, the cost barrier is one that must be addressed solely on the merits of an individual company's financial and market situation. It is not something this book can adequately address other than to recommend a balanced cost-benefit versus Risk approach.

The final barrier to successful Knowledge Management implementation is lack of need. The interesting point about this particular barrier is that on an estimated percentage basis, it is the least likely to keep a company from deploying a Knowledge Management solution, because the genuine need to manage corporate knowledge assets is widespread. As the requirement for market and technical innovation continues to increase, Knowledge Management will become not only best practice, but also an absolute necessity for the modern corporation.

# 7 CONTROL METHODS AND TECHNIQUES

## 7.1 Understanding the application's relationship to IT services

### 7.1.1 Relating applications to IT services

It is important to understand the relationship between an application and the IT service that it is meant to deliver. Only by doing this will an IT organisation be able to focus on the Critical Success Factors for the application and ensure that a quality service that meets the required SLA is delivered to Users.

This section focuses on the interrelationships between applications and IT services from three different perspectives. The first perspective focuses on the relationship between business functions and applications. The second perspective concerns the relationship and the management of that relationship among IT services, IT systems, and applications. For that purpose the Service Dependency Modelling technique is introduced. The third perspective takes the view of a single application going through the application lifecycle. Throughout the lifecycle quality attributes have to be monitored in order to align business requirements and the applications that support them.

### 7.1.2 Relating business functions to applications

The first relationship between a business function and IT is the IT service (see the Strategic Alignment Objectives Model (SAOM) in Figure 3.3). IT services are generally specified in Service Level Requirements (SLRs). These SLRs need to be specified in business terms, not in technical terms, in order to reflect the added value of the IT service in a Service Level Agreement (SLA). Most IT organisations that use SLAs to agree on a Quality of Service delivered by IT specify the SLRs in technical terms, such as CPU cycles, disk space, or bandwidth. Although agreeing on Service Levels is a good start, such SLRs as CPU cycles, disk space, and bandwidth are not reflecting the business value of the IT services delivered and do not facilitate linking applications with IT services or business functions.

IT services generally fulfil the information need of a business function. Often a sequence of IT services is needed to support the activities that are sequentially performed as a business function. Consider a billing and invoicing process from any service company. One of the first steps in preparing the invoice information is to collect the client's utilisation information on the delivered services. This information can vary from bought goods on a credit card, cash withdrawals, or network traffic on a data or voice line. An information system has been storing this information in a database. Therefore the first service is to collect that data from the database from a given invoicing period. The next service can, for instance, be to sort the utilisation figures on client name and to match the utilisation figures with the billing arrangements made with the client.

Applications and infrastructure components are needed in order to deliver the IT services defined and described. Applications fulfil a certain function in the business process or provide the information a business process needs. The application itself runs on an infrastructure that can be dedicated for the (set of) applications supporting a business process, but can also be shared with other applications supporting other business processes. If the business organisation can specify the Key Performance Indicators for the IT services supporting its business process, the IT services organisation can specify the SLRs and the technology requirements. Based on the technology requirements, the application, data, and infrastructure characteristics can be used to monitor the compliance with the agreed-upon Service Levels, and also to test compliance with changed and new information systems against the intended Service Levels.

In order to direct the service delivery activities within the IT services organisation, use Operational Level Agreements (OLAs) to define the operational requirements that IT systems need to meet. Using the relationship between IT services and applications in this way bridges the gap between the business and the IT services organisation.

To identify and measure the contribution of an application to a Service Level, one needs to understand how the application affects each identifiable function within the SLA. Examples of this could be the response time of a Customer entry screen to get information back and update the screen following the placement of an order. The SLA specifies a response time of, for example, less than five seconds for 99.9% of Customer transactions. The application relies on a browser, web server, host-based scripts, database server, stored procedures, and the underlying end-to-end infrastructure to deliver this Service Level. In achieving this Service Level it is clear that each of these applications makes a critical contribution to the system meeting this Service Level, and failure of any of them would affect the SLA for some or all clients.

### 7.1.3 Service Dependency Modelling

In order to understand and manage the reliance and criticality of an application within a system, it is important to understand how each application relates to others within the system, and also how this relationship affects other dependent systems.

One method of viewing the interdependency of applications is known as Service Dependency Modelling.

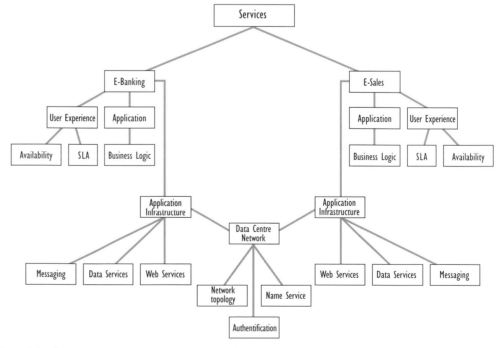

*Figure 7.1 – Typical entities captured in a Service Dependency Model*

Security Dependency Modelling is the process of graphically representing an IT service by describing the systems that create the service and the applications that make up the systems. The dependencies that exist between each of the applications are then identified and documented (see Figure 7.1).

Service Dependency Modelling is useful both on its own and when used with an enterprise Application Management system (examples of which include IBM Tivoli, HP Openview, CA Unicentre, and NetIQ Appmanager).

Service Dependency Modelling is an ideal process to aid the comprehensive understanding of a whole service. While Service Dependency Modelling can be done manually on paper, it is most effective when delivered by some automated method that can check and validate that the Service Dependency Modelling matches the state of the current configuration. Many of the vendors in this arena describe their tools as Application Management tools.

Some organisations looking at this subject also talk about service portfolios, and in most respects these can be talked about in the same vein as Service Dependency Modelling. Service portfolios focus on how one logically presents a set of applications to the User community in such a way that they meet a specific area of requirement or business function. It is also used to simplify the presentation of a cluster of applications that make up a system. Service Dependency Modelling can be considered as covering all the same areas as service portfolios, while adding the additional key area of application interdependencies.

An understanding of the structure and interdependencies that exist between each of these applications is presupposed when conducting Service Dependency Modelling. This also requires a list of business-prioritised functions and applications that must operate so that critical system functionality can be delivered and the SLA met. This will identify applications that are critical and must continue to operate for the system to function, and those applications that are desirable to have for Quality of Service, but not critical because they will not have an immediate effect on the Service Level. The application behaviour and failure scenarios are normally documented in pseudo-code. (Appendix C has more information on building a Service Dependency Model.)

## 7.2 Understanding the characteristics of the application

### 7.2.1 Understanding the relationship between quality and IT business value

Chapter 6 linked the applications to the IT services, where the IT services were linked to the key business drivers. Through this relationship, and the discussion in Chapter 3, the key business drivers are linked with the application characteristics of the applications used to fulfil the information needs of the business. The application characteristics can be seen as the quality attributes that are discussed in this chapter.

Much has been written about the subject of quality management of development projects and testing strategies. Literature and practices in this area focus on product quality of applications, with quality attributes as a measurable breakdown of quality. The main focus of these strategies is on quality management rather than on IT value to the business. Although some IT organisations have in various cases found ways to implement the quality management and testing strategies, many organisations have failed to align these strategies with the business value obtained from it.

There has never been a successful attempt to define quality, and many people have considered the term a 'container-type word'. That term is frequently used among pragmatic professionals to qualify terms that are rather meaningless unless better specified. Looking at various different definitions of quality, different words can be found, all saying that the consumer of a product determines the definition of quality. This provides the opportunity to link the quality attributes to the key business drivers of IT, as stated in Section 3.3. By linking the expected business value to the perception of quality, the IT services organisation has an instrument to manage the business value of IT by managing the quality attributes valued by the business.

---

**Definitions of quality**

'The total of characteristics of a software product that enables the software product to meet its expectations.'

'The whole of characteristics of a software product that are important for that software product to meet its agreed-upon and expected requirements.'

'Fitness for use.'

'Doing the right things at the right time once.'

---

In order to manage the business value of an application by its quality attributes, these quality attributes must be measurable throughout the lifecycle. For the quality attributes of an application to be measurable, the same rules apply as for the key business drivers. They should be unambiguous, verifiable, traceable, consistent, and, of course, agreed upon by each of the stakeholders playing a role in the application lifecycle. Much research has been done on the quality attributes of an application and how to measure them. Practices of these methods have mostly been a pragmatic implementation of these theories. This book addresses the pragmatic implementation of the theory instead of restating already published literature.

### 7.2.2 Using the quality attributes as a control tool

Three elements of the quality attributes need to be addressed by both business and IT. The first element is, of course, the definition of the quality attributes. Defining the quality attributes provides an unambiguous understanding of them that will be used by professionals throughout the lifecycle. The second and third elements involve agreeing on the way the quality attribute is going to be measured. This means defining the indicator and defining the test technique. The indicator makes the quality attribute unambiguous and traceable. Throughout the whole application lifecycle, the indicator tells what is meant by the quality attribute and how the definition of the quality attribute should be seen. The test technique determines how the quality is going to be evaluated. The three elements of quality attributes completely define the quality attribute and how people should understand it. Table 7.1 shows some examples of quality attributes and the three elements of the quality attribute.

*Table 7.1 – Examples of quality attributes*

### Availability

Definition: the extent to which a service is available for use by a business User

Indicator: Relative availability of the application as a percentage of the expected availability (RA)
*Measuring technique*
1. Determine the service period for the application
2. Determine the expected available hours during the service period (EA)
3. Measure the time an application is unavailable in hours (UA)
4. Calculate the relative availability by the formula: $RA = (EA - UA)/EA \times 100\%$

Indicator: Impacted availability based on the number of Users that could not work with the application (IA)
*Measuring technique*
1. Determine the number of Users (NU)
2. Measure the number of Users that were not able to use the application (IU)
3. Calculate the impacted availability by the formula: $IA = IU/NU \times 100\%$

Indicator: Absolute unavailability of the application as the number of mean time to repair (AU)
*Measuring technique*
1. Measure the time to repair for a specific application failure
2. Count the number of application failures
3. Calculate the number of application failures with a specific time to repair range
4. Classify the application failures as the number of downtimes with a time to repair of a certain range

### Recoverability

Definition: The speed with which an application can be repaired after failure

Indicator: Mean time to repair (MTTR)
*Measuring technique*
1. Measure the time to repair for each application failure (TTR)
2. Count the number of application failures that needed repair (AF)
3. Calculate the MTTR according to the formula: $MTTR = \sum TTR/AF$

If the quality attributes are defined to be used throughout the whole lifecycle, testing strategies can be developed to manage the IT value to the business by managing the quality attributes of the IT system. The testing strategies should be based on the risk any new development will bring to the existing and intended SLAs between the business and the IT services organisation. Considering the threat of not meeting a certain SLR, parties should estimate, using a pre-defined Risk Assessment, the risk that the lack of a certain quality attribute will result in not meeting the existing or intended SLAs. This Risk Assessment will determine the acceptance criteria set by each of the stakeholders in the application lifecycle. The acceptance criteria are the quality attributes that were deemed most important to evaluate during the test activities, set with a norm to which the quality attribute should comply. The definition of the acceptance criteria based on a Risk Assessment for deploying a new or changed IT system is shown in Figure 7.2.

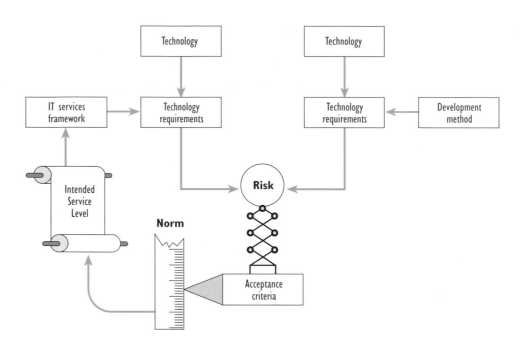

*Figure 7.2 – Determining the acceptance criteria*

### 7.2.3 Testing applications to intended business value

To define the test plan, a test leader can identify the relevant quality attributes for the applications that need to be tested. Although the quality attributes are the binding factor for testing the applications, multiple parties, each having different objectives, will determine the quality attributes and the norm those quality attributes need to meet during testing. It is the test leader's challenge to supervise the selection of quality attributes with their norm. This will not always be an easy task, since some quality attributes are conflicting and some are hard to quantify. For instance, the business might want to have an adjustable application, which is hard to quantify and which will have a negative influence on the performance of that application. This example not only demonstrates possible conflicts between quality attributes, but also puts the use of quality attributes in the perspective of the intended business value. The test leader should not only agree on the quality attributes and their norm, but also on what measures should be taken if quality attributes are not met during testing.

Selection of quality attributes can be made using simple tables to identify the importance of certain quality attributes with regard to the applications that need to be tested. The importance of certain quality attributes for a given business process can be evaluated against the importance of certain applications to support that business process. In this way a weighted factor can be obtained for a given quality attribute in relation to the applications that need to be tested. Based on the relative importance and the defined test techniques of a quality attribute, a selection of test techniques can be made. The more important a quality attribute and its related application are, the more intensive test techniques can be used. The test leader can now document the test techniques in a test plan. The test plan will state what tests will be performed, when they will be performed, and what the expected result of that test should be. The test plan will also define the responsibilities during testing. This means that the test plan will state who is performing the tests and who is accepting the results after testing. In this way the test plan can be used as a project completion criterion to which all stakeholders can agree. An example of the test strategy table is shown in Table 7.2.

*Table 7.2 – Test strategy matrix*

| | Imp. | Application 1 | Application 2 | ... | Application n |
|---|---|---|---|---|---|
| | | 2 | 3 | .. | 1 |
| Responsiveness | 3 | 6 | 9 | .. | 3 |
| Throughput | 1 | 2 | 3 | .. | 1 |
| Installability | 2 | 4 | 6 | .. | 2 |
| ..... | .. | .. | .. | .. | .. |
| Durability | 3 | 6 | 9 | .. | 3 |

The test plan should do more than specify dynamic testing after the applications are built. Static testing can be used to verify the design and test documentation during the application lifecycle. Static tests are used to verify correctness and completeness of all development and test work products against predecessor work products, business and technical expertise, and organisation standards. If static tests are correctly used, errors will be found much earlier in the lifecycle and closer to the source. It will reduce the development and testing time by minimising rework.

It is best to use a dedicated test team to perform the sort of test strategy discussed in this section. The governance of the test team can vary. An organisation can choose to have the test leader report to the project owner or the project manager. Since the project owner is ultimately responsible for accepting the applications, the test team can be separate from the project and test on behalf of all accepting parties. The test team can also report to the project manager, since the test plan, and the defined acceptance criteria in the plan, form the project completion criteria. These project completion criteria define the moment a project manager can be discharged from the project.

# 8 CONCLUDING REMARKS

Many IT practitioners understand that Application Management is a discipline which needs management attention and that there are best practices which can be shared and implemented. However, few practitioners have a common understanding of what Application Management is, and what should be addressed when discussing, planning and implementing Application Management.

This book has defined the management activities and outlined approaches to managing applications as corporate assets. However, Application Management needs to be put in a wider context to ensure that benefits are achieved during and after its implementation. The benefits of Application Management can be found in the linking together of disciplines such as project management, Application Management and ICT Service Management, all topics that are covered extensively in OGC guidance.

## 8.1 Benefits of Application Management

It may be questioned whether the benefits identified are due to the implementation of Application Management or to the implementation of the other disciplines mentioned earlier, for example project management. However, there are a number of direct benefits to be realised by implementing Application Management.

- By managing applications from different perspectives during their lifecycle, investments in IT can be viewed objectively, for instance, IT seen from the perspective of a cost centre, service centre, profit centre or investment centre. From a cost centre perspective high levels of investments in IT could be viewed as a waste of good money that ought to be invested in other parts of the company. However, from a profit or investment centre perspective, investing insufficient resources in business critical applications could result in loss of business revenue and even the company's good name.

- The use of the Strategic Alignment Objectives Model (SAOM) can help IT services organisations to communicate and justify their business value, and manage the IT Infrastructure in alignment with the key business drivers of the business functions they support. The SAOM is also useful for business functions to manage IT from a business perspective.

- Managing applications as corporate assets will focus management attention on the service delivery capabilities rather than on the short-term project implementation. This focus will stimulate organisations to implement application portfolio management, and to assess and adjust organisational capabilities in order to manage applications throughout their use.

- Linking the key business drivers to the application requirements, or quality attributes, enables organisations to design strategies to test applications in relation to their intended value to the business.

- Linking key business drivers to team goals and the use of overlapping goals in order to share responsibilities will ensure a more long-term business-driven culture in the application development and IT services organisation. In this way the value of an application is tested, rather than the application itself.

## 8.2 Potential implementation pitfalls

Although there are many advantages in practising Application Management, the use of Application Management best practices in an immature organisation will only lead to extra management costs, without delivering any added value to the business. If Application Management is improperly implemented it is likely to lead to the creation of an unnecessary administrative burden, with few tangible or intangible benefits. To avoid such a scenario then the following considerations should be taken into account when planning to implement Application Management:

- Do not try to implement the SAOM before stable service delivery to the business is established. Experience shows that most business functions are not willing to discuss added value or strategic issues when the availability and flexibility of the current IT services are poor.

- It is of little use to implement Application Management best practices, overlapping other disciplines like IT Service Management and application development, if these other disciplines have not reached a sufficient level of maturity. It is not possible to implement inter-process dependencies and management controls if the individual processes have no measurements and controls.

- Before implementing an application portfolio it is important to have mature Configuration Management, Release Management and software Configuration Management processes. There are few benefits to be gained from managing the IT investments from a business point of view if the assets themselves are not managed at an IT level.

- The implementation of Application Management should not be confused with the introduction of other disciplines such as Service Level Management and testing. If an organisation attempts to introduce a number of disciplines under the banner of Application Management then the costs and time implications will be extremely high and the implementation may be called to a halt.

- It will not be possible to determine whether process execution has been enhanced through implementing Knowledge Management unless processes have reached a level of maturity at which efficiency and effectiveness are constantly measured.

## 8.3 Application evolution

Assuming Application Management is implemented successfully within the organisation, it is important to recognise that it interacts with other processes. Improvements to these processes would need to be made in conjunction with improvements to Application Management if the maturity level of the overall ICT environment is to be raised.

Some of the key actions that can result in synergistic improvements in Application Management are presented in this section.

### 8.3.1 Improving the Change Management process

Change Management is critical to an effective Application Management process. A comprehensive, end-to-end process for managing changes begins with the recognition and assessment of all changes to the business in terms of both risk and impact. Changes are planned, monitored and controlled and the lifecycle is completed with their full implementation and evaluation. To improve the maturity level of the Change Management process within an organisation the following principles should be adhered to:

- Appoint a Change Manager with a broad business perspective, preferably a senior business manager with the power to reject, veto or approve requested changes. This is particularly important when the demand for change exceeds the capability to deliver changes, so that business priorities are recognised and agreed.

- Produce, agree and publish a Change Management Strategy for Change initiators which outlines:
    - explicit responsibilities for change authorisation
    - change evaluation, prioritisation and categorisation criteria
    - strategies for implementing small or minor changes, larger run/build time changes, changes with major impact, urgent and emergency repair type changes
    - the Release strategy for scheduled changes
      change testing and implementation procedures
    - post implementation review, management reporting and auditing of changes.

- Produce adequate plans for changes reflecting both risk and impact assessments.

- Register all Requests For Changes (RFCs) centrally and ensure that they are formally authorised by both IT and business management.

- Ensure that the Change Advisory Board (CAB) plays an active rather than passive role in Change Management. The CAB should assess changes for their effect on the IT Infrastructure and User service and the resources required to implement changes.

- Have formal post-implementation reviews of changes which adequately involve User representatives, to ensure that:
    - the established change had the desired effect with no unexpected side-effects
    - Users are content with the results
    - resources used to implement the changes were as planned.

- All changes are closed and the Change log updated to reflect whether the change implementation was satisfactory or abandoned, with any pending issues documented.

- Establish the history of all changes and review the potential effect of proposed changes on SLAs.

- Provide summaries of changes to Service Management and Customers.

### 8.3.2 Improving the testing process

Implement improvements in the approach to testing changes. Of particular importance in the evolution of applications is the approach to regression testing to ensure that enhancement and other maintenance activities are not adversely affecting the application and overall service. Some recommendations for improving the approach to testing include:

- Use standard (tested) components and prototyping to eliminate many of the operational, User interface and usability defects that can be introduced when performing changes

- Plan unit, integration and system testing to target functionality performance, supportability, reliability/availability, security and maintainability

- Ensure that change and back-out procedures are fully tested

- Isolate the test environment from any 'live' environments and ensure that test environments are isolated from each other where necessary

- Where tested changes can only be partially tested in a test environment ensure that they are implemented when they will least impact the 'live services'.

### 8.3.3    Improving the Release Management process

From the Application Management perspective, there are two key assumptions that relate to Release Management. The first is that the rate of accumulation of change requests could possibly exceed the resources available to deal with them and consequently a controlled Release cycle is an efficient way to handle changes to applications. The second is that sufficient resources are made available to allow a significant volume of changes to be incorporated into a Release with relatively short intervals between Releases.

A balance must be achieved between a rapid response to User Requests For Changes and the need to maintain effective deployment of resources on maintenance activities. It is not feasible to respond immediately to every User change request, nor is it always desirable, as impacts must be assessed and potentially conflicting requests identified and resolved. Packaging changes into releases enables effective resource utilisation. However, in a maintenance scenario releases cannot be so far apart that Users have to wait an unreasonable length of time for new or modified functions that are necessary to the business.

The following recommendations are aimed at improving the Release Management process in a maintenance environment:

- Release Management should be used for large or critical hardware and software roll-outs

- Related sets of changes should be bundled together into manageable sets and, where possible, implemented as all or part of a Release

- A high-level Release schedule should be produced and agreed with the business

- A plan is required for each Release, which includes high-level test plans and acceptance criteria for each Release

- All software, parameters, test data and run-time software required for a Release must be under Configuration Management control

- Back-out procedures for the Release must be tested and Release acceptance must be performed in a controlled environment

- Customer expectations need to be managed during the planning and roll-out of Releases

- Metrics should be in place to monitor the effectiveness of the Release Management process, for example, Releases built and implemented on schedule, low incidence of Release back-out.

The Change Management and Release Management processes are described in detail within the ITIL book, *Service Support*. Testing is an integral part of both Application Management and ICT Infrastructure Management and further details relating to the testing of ICT infrastructure components can be found in the *ICT Infrastructure Management* book.

For an overall approach to continuous improvement of ITIL processes, the reader is advised to refer to ITIL: *Planning to Implement Service Management*.

# 9 BIBLIOGRAPHY

## 9.1 References

Please note that the entries in this section are given in alphabetical order of title.

*Assessing the Strategic Value of Information Technology: Planning Perspectives for Senior Executives*
The Economist Intelligent Unit and IBM Global Services 1999
The Economist Intelligent Unit, New York
ISBN 0-85058-481-7

*The Balanced Scorecard: Translating Strategy into Action*
Robert S. Kaplan, David P. Norton 1996
Harvard Business School Press, Boston
ISBN 0-87584-651-3

*The Business Perspective*
OGC
Available from TSO (The Stationery Office), www.tso.co.uk
ISBN 0-11-330894-9

*Design Patterns, Elements of Reusable Object-oriented Software*
Erich Gamma, Richard Helm, Ralph Johnson, John Vlissides 1995
Addison Wesley Professional Computing Series, Addison Wesley Publishing Company,
Reading, MA
ISBN 0-201-63361-2

*Dynamics of Software Development*
Jim McCarthy 1995
Microsoft Press
ISBN 1-55615-823-8

*ICT Infrastructure Management*
OGC
Available from TSO, www.tso.co.uk
ISBN 0-11-330865-5

*IS Management Guides series*
OGC, www.ogc.gov.uk
Format

*Management of Risk: Guidance for Practitioners*
OGC
Available from TSO, www.tso.co.uk

*Managing Successful Projects with PRINCE2, Revised Edition*
OGC 2002
Available from TSO, www.tso.co.uk
ISBN 0-11-330891-4

*Managing the Software Process*
Watts S. Humphrey 1989
SEI Series in Software Engineering, Addison Wesley Publishing Company, Reading, MA
ISBN 0-201-18095-2

*Planning to Implement Service Management*
OGC 2002
Available from TSO, www.tso.co.uk
ISBN 0-11-330877-9

*Security Management*
OGC
Available from TSO, www.tso.co.uk
ISBN 0-11-330014-X

*Service Delivery*
OGC 2001
Available from TSO, www.tso.co.uk
ISBN 0-11-330017-4

*Service Support*
OGC 2000
Available from TSO, www.tso.co.uk
ISBN 0-11-330015-8

*Strategic Alignment: Leveraging Information Technology for Transforming Organisations*
J.C. Henderson, N. Venkatraman 1993
IBM Systems Journal, Vol. 32, No. 1, pp. 4-16


## 9.2    Other sources

British Standards Institution
Website at www.bsi.org.uk

Capability Maturity Model for Software (CMM or SW-CMM)
Website at www.sei.cmu.edu/cmm

European Foundation for Quality Management
Website at www.efqm.org

ISO9000 Information Forum
Website at www.iso-9000.co.uk

Office of Government Commerce (OGC)
Website at www.ogc.gov.uk

W. Edwards Deming Institute (The)
Website at www.deming.org

# APPENDIX A LIST OF ACRONYMS AND GLOSSARY

## A.1 Acronyms

| | |
|---|---|
| AMDB | Availability Management Database |
| AMS | Application Management Specification |
| API | Application Program Interface |
| ARCI | Accountability, Responsibility, Consulted, Informed |
| BIA | Business Impact Analysis |
| BPR | Business Process Re-engineering |
| BSI | British Standards Institute |
| CAB | Change Advisory Board |
| CAB/EC | Change Advisory Board Emergency Committee |
| CASE | Computer-Aided Systems Engineering |
| CBT | Computer Based Training |
| CDB | Capacity (Management) Database |
| CFIA | Component Failure Impact Analysis |
| CI | Configuration Item |
| CIO | Chief Information Officer |
| CMDB | Configuration Management Database |
| CMM | Capability Maturity Model |
| COBIT | Control Objectives for Information and Related Technology |
| CSF | Critical Success Factor |
| CSIP | Continuous Service Improvement Programme |
| CSS | Customer Satisfaction Survey |
| CTO | Chief Technology Officer |
| DMI | Desktop Management Instrumentation |
| DMTF | Distributed Management Task Force |
| DSL | Definitive Software Library |
| EFQM | European Foundation for Quality Management |
| ERP | Enterprise Resource Planning |

| | |
|---|---|
| EXIN | Examination Institute for Information Science |
| ICT | Information and Communication Technology |
| ICTSG | ICT Steering Group |
| ISEB | Information Systems Examination Board |
| ISG | IT Steering Group |
| ISO | International Standards Organisation |
| IT | Information Technology |
| ITIL | Information Technology Infrastructure Library |
| ITSC | IT Service Continuity |
| ITSM | Information Technology Service Management |
| *it*SMF | IT Service Management Forum |
| IVR | Interactive Voice Response |
| KPI | Key Performance Indicator |
| MAC | Movements, Additions and Changes |
| MTBF | Mean Time Between Failures |
| MTBSI | Mean Time Between System Incidents |
| MTTR | Mean Time To Repair |
| OGC | Office of Government Commerce |
| OLA | Operational Level Agreement |
| PIR | Post Implementation Review |
| PMF | Process Maturity Framework |
| R and D | Research and Development |
| RFC | Request For Change |
| SEI | Software Engineering Institute |
| SLA | Service Level Agreement |
| SLM | Service Level Management |
| SLR | Service Level Requirement |
| SMART | Specific, Measurable, Achievable, Realistic, Time-related |
| SOCITM | Society of Council IT Managers  SOR Statement Of Requirements |
| SPI | Software Process Improvement |
| SPICE | Software Process Improvement and Capability dEtermination |
| SPMF | Service management Process Maturity Framework |
| SWOT | Strengths, Weaknesses, Opportunities and Threats |

| TCO | Total Cost of Ownership |
| TQM | Total Quality Management |
| TTO | Transfer To Operation |
| WMI | Windows Management Instrumentation |
| WORM | Write Once, Read Many (optical read-only disks) |

## A.2 Glossary

**absorbed overhead**

Overhead which, by means of absorption rates, is included in costs of specific products or saleable services, in a given period of time. Under- or over-absorbed overhead: the difference between overhead cost incurred and overhead cost absorbed: it may be split into its two constituent parts for control purposes.

**absorption costing**

A principle whereby fixed as well as variable costs are allotted to cost units and total overheads are absorbed according to activity level. The term may be applied where production costs only, or costs of all functions are so allotted.

**action lists**

Defined actions, allocated to recovery teams and individuals, within a phase of a plan. These are supported by reference data.

**alert**

Warning that an Incident has occurred.

**alert phase**

The first phase of a business continuity plan in which initial emergency procedures and damage assessments are activated.

**allocated cost**

A cost that can be directly identified with a business unit.

**application portfolio**

An information system containing key attributes of applications deployed in a company. Application portfolios are used as tools to manage the business value of an application throughout its lifecycle.

**apportioned cost**

A cost that is shared by a number of business units (an indirect cost). This cost must be shared out between these units on an equitable basis.

**asset**

Component of a business process. Assets can include people, accommodation, computer systems, networks, paper records, fax machines, etc.

**asynchronous/synchronous**

In a communications sense, the ability to transmit each character as a self-contained unit of information, without additional timing information. This method of transmitting data is sometimes called start/stop. Synchronous working involves the use of timing information to allow transmission of data, which is normally done in blocks. Synchronous transmission is usually more efficient than the asynchronous method.

**availability**

Ability of a component or service to perform its required function at a stated instant or over a stated period of time. It is usually expressed as the availability ratio, i.e. the proportion of time that the service is actually available for use by the Customers within the agreed service hours.

**Balanced Scorecard**

An aid to organisational performance management. It helps to focus not only on the financial targets but also on the internal processes, Customers and learning and growth issues.

**baseline**

A snapshot or a position which is recorded. Although the position may be updated later, the baseline remains unchanged and available as a reference of the original state and as a comparison against the current position (PRINCE2).

**baseline security**

The security level adopted by the IT organisation for its own security and from the point of view of good 'due diligence'.

**baselining**

Process by which the quality and cost-effectiveness of a service is assessed, usually in advance of a change to the service. Baselining usually includes comparison of the service before and after the change or analysis of trend information. The term benchmarking is usually used if the comparison is made against other enterprises.

**bridge**

Equipment and techniques used to match circuits to each other ensuring minimum transmission impairment.

**BS7799**

The British standard for Information Security Management. This standard provides a comprehensive set of controls comprising best practices in information security.

**budgeting**

Budgeting is the process of predicting and controlling the spending of money within the organisation and consists of a periodic negotiation cycle to set budgets (usually annual) and the day-to-day monitoring of current budgets.

**build**

The final stage in producing a usable configuration. The process involves taking one of more input Configuration Items and processing them (building them) to create one or more output Configuration Items, e.g. software compile and load.

**business function**

A business unit within an organisation, e.g. a department, division, branch.

**business process**

A group of business activities undertaken by an organisation in pursuit of a common goal. Typical business processes include receiving orders, marketing services, selling products, delivering services, distributing products, invoicing for services, accounting for money received. A business process usually depends upon several business functions for support, e.g. IT, personnel, and accommodation. A business process rarely operates in isolation, i.e. other business processes will depend on it and it will depend on other processes.

**business recovery objective**

The desired time within which business processes should be recovered, and the minimum staff, assets and services required within this time.

**business recovery plan framework**

A template business recovery plan (or set of plans) produced to allow the structure and proposed contents to be agreed before the detailed business recovery plan is produced.

**business recovery plans**

Documents describing the roles, responsibilities and actions necessary to resume business processes following a business disruption.

**business recovery team**

A defined group of personnel with a defined role and subordinate range of actions to facilitate recovery of a business function or process.

**business unit**

A segment of the business entity by which both revenues are received and expenditure is caused or controlled, such revenues and expenditure being used to evaluate segmental performance.

**Capital Costs**

Typically those costs applying to the physical (substantial) assets of the organisation. Traditionally this was the accommodation and machinery necessary to produce the enterprise's product. Capital Costs are the purchase or major enhancement of fixed assets, for example, computer equipment (building and plant) and are often also referred to as 'one-off' costs.

**capital investment appraisal**

The process of evaluating proposed investment in specific fixed assets and the benefits to be obtained from their acquisition. The techniques used in the evaluation can be summarised as non-discounting methods (i.e. simple payback), return on capital employed and discounted cashflow methods (i.e. yield, net present value and discounted payback).

**capitalisation**

The process of identifying major expenditure as Capital, whether there is a substantial asset or not, to reduce the impact on the current financial year of such expenditure. The most common item for this to be applied to is software, whether developed in-house or purchased.

**category**

Classification of a group of Configuration Items, Change documents or problems.

**Change**

The addition, modification or removal of approved, supported or baselined hardware, network, software, application, environment, system, desktop build or associated documentation.

**Change Advisory Board (CAB)**

> A group of people who can give expert advice to Change Management on the implementation of changes. This board is likely to be made up of representatives from all areas within IT and representatives from business units.

**Change Authority**

> A group that is given the authority to approve Change, e.g. by the project board. Sometimes referred to as the Configuration Board.

**Change Control**

> The procedure to ensure that all changes are controlled, including the submission, analysis, decision-making, approval, implementation and post-implementation of the change.

**Change document**

> Request For Change, Change Control form, Change order, Change record.

**Change history**

> Auditable information that records, for example, what was done, when it was done, by whom and why.

**Change log**

> A log of Requests For Change raised during the project, showing information on each Change, its evaluation, what decisions have been made and its current status, e.g. Raised, Reviewed, Approved, Implemented, Closed.

**Change Management**

> Process of controlling changes to the infrastructure or any aspect of services, in a controlled manner, enabling approved changes with minimum disruption.

**Change record**

> A record containing details of which CIs are affected by an authorised change (planned or implemented) and how.

**charging**

> The process of establishing charges in respect of business units, and raising the relevant invoices for recovery from Customers.

**classification**

> Process of formally grouping Configuration Items by type, e.g. software, hardware, documentation, environment, application.

> Process of formally identifying changes by type e.g. project scope change request, validation change request, infrastructure change request.

> Process of formally identifying Incidents, problems and Known Errors by origin, symptoms and cause.

**closure**

> When the Customer is satisfied that an Incident has been resolved.

**cold stand-by**

> See 'gradual recovery'.

**command, control and communications**

The processes by which an organisation retains overall coordination of its recovery effort during invocation of business recovery plans.

**Computer-Aided Systems Engineering (CASE)**

A software tool for programmers. It provides help in the planning, analysis, design and documentation of computer software.

**Configuration baseline**

Configuration of a product or system established at a specific point in time, which captures both the structure and details of the product or system, and enables that product or system to be rebuilt at a later date.

A snapshot or a position which is recorded. Although the position may be updated later, the baseline remains unchanged and available as a reference of the original state and as a comparison against the current position (PRINCE2).

See also 'baseline'.

**Configuration control**

Activities comprising the control of changes to Configuration Items after formally establishing its configuration documents. It includes the evaluation, coordination, approval or rejection of changes. The implementation of changes includes changes, deviations and waivers that impact on the configuration.

**Configuration documentation**

Documents that define requirements, system design, build, production, and verification for a Configuration Item.

**Configuration identification**

Activities that determine the product structure, the selection of Configuration Items, and the documentation of the Configuration Item's physical and functional characteristics including interfaces and subsequent changes. It includes the allocation of identification characters or numbers to the Configuration Items and their documents. It also includes the unique numbering of Configuration control forms associated with changes and Problems.

**Configuration Item (CI)**

Component of an infrastructure – or an item, such as a Request For Change, associated with an infrastructure – which is (or is to be) under the control of Configuration Management. CIs may vary widely in complexity, size and type – from an entire system (including all hardware, software and documentation) to a single module or a minor hardware component.

**Configuration Management**

The process of identifying and defining the Configuration Items in a system, recording and reporting the status of Configuration Items and Requests For Change, and verifying the completeness and correctness of Configuration Items.

**Configuration Management Database (CMDB)**

A database which contains all relevant details of each CI and details of the important relationships between CIs.

**Configuration Management plan**

Document setting out the organisation and procedures for the Configuration Management of a specific product, project, system, support group or service.

**Configuration Management Tool (CM Tool)**

A software product providing automatic support for Change, Configuration or version control.

**Configuration Structure**

A hierarchy of all the CIs that comprise a configuration.

**Contingency Planning**

Planning to address unwanted occurrences that may happen at a later time. Traditionally, the term has been used to refer to planning for the recovery of IT systems rather than entire business processes.

**Continuous Service Improvement Programme**

An ongoing formal programme undertaken within an organisation to identify and introduce measurable improvements within a specified work area or work process.

**cost**

The amount of expenditure (actual or notional) incurred on, or attributable to, a specific activity or business unit.

**cost-effectiveness**

Ensuring that there is a proper balance between the Quality of Service on the one side and expenditure on the other. Any investment that increases the costs of providing IT services should always result in enhancement to service quality or quantity.

**cost management**

All the procedures, tasks and deliverables that are needed to fulfil an organisation's costing and charging requirements.

**cost of failure**

A technique used to evaluate and measure the cost of failed actions and activities. It can be measured as a total within a period or an average per failure. An example would be 'the cost of failed changes per month' or 'the average cost of a failed change'.

**cost unit**

In the context of CSBC the cost unit is a functional cost unit which establishes standard cost per workload element of activity, based on calculated activity ratios converted to cost ratios.

**costing**

The process of identifying the costs of the business and of breaking them down and relating them to the various activities of the organisation.

**countermeasure**

A check or restraint on the service designed to enhance security by reducing the risk of an attack (by reducing either the threat or the vulnerability), reducing the impact of an attack, detecting the occurrence of an attack and/or assisting in the recovery from an attack.

**crisis management**

> The processes by which an organisation manages the wider impact of a disaster, such as adverse media coverage.

**Critical Success Factor (CSF)**

> A measure of success or maturity of a project or process. It can be a state, a deliverable or a milestone. An example of a CSF would be 'the production of an overall technology strategy'.

**Customer**

> Recipient of the service; usually the Customer management has responsibility for the cost of the service, either directly through charging or indirectly in terms of demonstrable business need.

**data transfer time**

> The length of time taken for a block or sector of data to be read from or written to an I/O device, such as a disk or tape.

**Definitive Software Library (DSL)**

> The library in which the definitive authorised versions of all software CIs are stored and protected. It is a physical library or storage repository where master copies of software versions are placed. This one logical storage area may in reality consist of one or more physical software libraries or filestores. They should be separate from development and test filestore areas. The DSL may also include a physical store to hold master copies of bought-in software, e.g. fireproof safe. Only authorised software should be accepted into the DSL, strictly controlled by Change and Release Management.

> The DSL exists not directly because of the needs of the Configuration Management process, but as a common base for the Release Management and Configuration Management processes.

**Delta Release**

> A Delta, or partial, Release is one that includes only those CIs within the Release unit that have actually changed or are new since the last full or Delta Release. For example, if the Release unit is the program, a Delta Release contains only those modules that have changed, or are new, since the last Full Release of the program or the last Delta Release of the modules.

> See also 'Full Release'.

**dependency**

> The reliance, either direct or indirect, of one process or activity upon another.

**depreciation**

> The loss in value of an asset due to its use and/or the passage of time. The annual depreciation charge in accounts represents the amount of capital assets used up in the accounting period. It is charged in the cost accounts to ensure that the cost of capital equipment is reflected in the unit costs of the services provided using the equipment. There are various methods of calculating depreciation for the period, but the Treasury usually recommends the use of current cost asset valuation as the basis for the depreciation charge.

**differential charging**

> Charging business Customers different rates for the same work, typically to dampen demand or to generate revenue for spare capacity. This can also be used to encourage off-peak or night-time running.

**direct cost**

> A cost that is incurred for, and can be traced in full to a product, service, cost centre or department. This is an allocated cost. Direct costs are direct materials, direct wages and direct expenses.

> See also 'indirect cost'.

**disaster recovery planning**

> A series of processes that focus only upon the recovery processes, principally in response to physical disasters, that are contained within BCM.

**discounted cashflow**

> An evaluation of the future net cashflows generated by a capital project by discounting them to their present-day value. The two methods most commonly used are:

> yield method, for which the calculation determines the internal rate of return (IRR) in the form of a percentage

> net present value (NPV) method, in which the discount rate is chosen and the answer is a sum of money.

**discounting**

> The offering to business Customers of reduced rates for the use of off-peak resources.

> See also 'surcharging'.

**disk cache controller**

> Memory that is used to store blocks of data that have been read from the disk devices connected to them. If a subsequent I/O requires a record that is still resident in the cache memory, it will be picked up from there, thus saving another physical I/O.

**downtime**

> Total period that a service or component is not operational, within agreed service times.

**duplex (full and half)**

> Full duplex line/channel allows simultaneous transmission in both directions. Half duplex line/channel is capable of transmitting in both directions, but only in one direction at a time.

**echoing**

> A reflection of the transmitted signal from the receiving end; a visual method of error detection in which the signal from the originating device is looped back to that device so that it can be displayed.

**elements of cost**

> The constituent parts of costs according to the factors upon which expenditure is incurred viz., materials, labour and expenses.

**End User**

> See 'User'.

**environment**

A collection of hardware, software, network communications and procedures that work together to provide a discrete type of computer service. There may be one or more environments on a physical platform, e.g. test, production. An environment has unique features and characteristics that dictate how they are administered in similar, yet diverse manners.

**Expert User**

See 'Super User'.

**external target**

One of the measures against which a delivered IT service is compared, expressed in terms of the Customer's business.

**financial year**

An accounting period covering 12 consecutive months. In the public sector this financial year generally coincides with the fiscal year which runs from 1 April to 31 March.

**first-line support**

Service Desk call logging and resolution (on agreed areas, for example MS Word).

**first time fix rate**

Commonly used metric, used to define Incidents resolved at the first point of contact between a Customer and the Service Provider, without delay or referral, generally by a front line support group such as a help desk or Service Desk. First time fixes are a sub-set of remote fixes.

**Forward Schedule of Changes (FSC)**

Contains details of all the changes approved for implementation and their proposed implementation dates. It should be agreed with the Customers and the business, Service Level Management, the Service Desk and Availability Management. Once agreed, the Service Desk should communicate to the User community at large any planned additional downtime arising from implementing the changes, using the most effective methods available.

**full cost**

The total cost of all the resources used in supplying a service, i.e. the sum of the direct costs of producing the output, a proportional share of overhead costs and any selling and distribution expenses. Both cash costs and notional (non-cash) costs should be included, including the cost of capital.

See also 'Total Cost of Ownership'.

**Full Release**

All components of the Release unit are built, tested, distributed and implemented together.

See also 'Delta Release'.

**Gateway**

Equipment which is used to interface networks so that a terminal on one network can communicate with services or a terminal on another.

**gradual recovery**

Previously called 'cold stand-by', this is applicable to organisations that do not need

125

immediate restoration of business processes and can function for a period of up to 72 hours, or longer, without a re-establishment of full IT facilities. This may include the provision of empty accommodation fully equipped with power, environmental controls and local network cabling infrastructure, telecommunications connections, and available in a disaster situation for an organisation to install its own computer equipment.

**hard charging**

Descriptive of a situation where, within an organisation, actual funds are transferred from the Customer to the IT organisation in payment for the delivery of IT services.

**hard fault**

The situation in a virtual memory system when the required page of code or data that a program was using has been redeployed by the operating system for some other purpose. This means that another piece of memory must be found to accommodate the code or data, and will involve physical reading/writing of pages to the page file.

**host**

A host computer comprises the central hardware and software resources of a computer complex, e.g. CPU, memory, channels, disk and magnetic tape I/O subsystems plus operating and applications software. The term is used to denote all non-network items.

**hot stand-by**

See 'immediate recovery'.

**ICT**

The convergence of Information Technology, Telecommunications and Data Networking Technologies into a single technology.

**immediate recovery**

Previously called 'hot stand-by', provides for the immediate restoration of services following any irrecoverable Incident. It is important to distinguish between the previous definition of 'hot stand-by' and 'immediate recovery'. Hot stand-by typically referred to availability of services within a short timescale such as 2 or 4 hours whereas immediate recovery implies the instant availability of services.

**impact**

Measure of the business criticality of an Incident. Often equal to the extent to which an Incident leads to distortion of agreed or expected Service Levels.

**impact analysis**

The identification of critical business processes, and the potential damage or loss that may be caused to the organisation resulting from a disruption to those processes. Business impact analysis identifies:

-  the form the loss or damage will take
- how that degree of damage or loss is likely to escalate with time following an Incident
- the minimum staffing, facilities and services needed to enable business processes to continue to operate at a minimum acceptable level
- the time within which they should be recovered.

The time within which full recovery of the business processes is to be achieved is also identified.

**impact code**

>   Simple code assigned to Incidents and problems, reflecting the degree of impact upon the Customer's business processes. It is the major means of assigning priority for dealing with Incidents.

**impact scenario**

>   Description of the type of impact on the business that could follow a business disruption. Usually related to a business process and will always refer to a period of time, e.g. Customer services will be unable to operate for two days.

**Incident**

>   Any event which is not part of the standard operation of a service and which causes, or may cause, an interruption to, or a reduction in, the quality of that service.

**Incident Control**

>   The process of identifying, recording, classifying and progressing Incidents until affected services return to normal operation.

**indirect cost**

>   A cost incurred in the course of making a product providing a service or running a cost centre or department, but which cannot be traced directly and in full to the product, service or department, because it has been incurred for a number of cost centres or cost units. These costs are apportioned to cost centres/cost units. Indirect costs are also referred to as overheads.

>   See also 'direct cost'.

**Informed Customer**

>   An individual, team or group with functional responsibility within an organisation for ensuring that spend on IS/IT is directed to best effect, i.e. that the business is receiving value for money and continues to achieve the most beneficial outcome. In order to fulfil its role the 'Informed' Customer function must gain clarity of vision in relation to the business plans and assure that suitable strategies are devised and maintained for achieving business goals.

>   The 'Informed' Customer function ensures that the needs of the business are effectively translated into a business requirements specification, that IT investment is both efficiently and economically directed, and that progress towards effective business solutions is monitored. The 'Informed' Customer should play an active role in the procurement process, e.g. in relation to business case development, and also in ensuring that the services and solutions obtained are used effectively within the organisation to achieve maximum business benefits. The term is often used in relation to the outsourcing of IT/IS. Sometimes also called 'Intelligent Customer'.

**interface**

>   Physical or functional interaction at the boundary between Configuration Items.

**intermediate recovery**

>   Previously called 'warm stand-by', typically involves the re-establishment of the critical systems and services within a 24 to 72 hour period, and is used by organisations that need to recover IT facilities within a predetermined time to prevent impacts to the business process.

**internal target**

> One of the measures against which supporting processes for the IT service are compared. Usually expressed in technical terms relating directly to the underpinning service being measured.

**invocation (of business recovery plans)**

> Putting business recovery plans into operation after a business disruption.

**invocation (of stand-by arrangements)**

> Putting stand-by arrangements into operation as part of business recovery activities.

**invocation and recovery phase**

> The second phase of a business recovery plan.

**ISO9001**

> The internationally accepted set of standards concerning quality management systems.

**IT accounting**

> The set of processes that enable the IT organisation to account fully for the way money is spent (particularly the ability to identify costs by Customer, by service and by activity).

**IT directorate**

> The part of an organisation charged with developing and delivering the IT services.

**IT Infrastructure**

> The sum of an organisation's IT related hardware, software, data telecommunication facilities, procedures and documentation.

**IT service**

> A described set of facilities, IT and non-IT, supported by the IT Service Provider that fulfils one or more needs of the Customer and that is perceived by the Customer as a coherent whole.

**IT Service Provider**

> The role of IT Service Provider is performed by any organisational units, whether internal or external, that deliver and support IT services to a Customer.

**ITIL**

> The OGC IT Infrastructure Library – a set of guides on the management and provision of operational IT services.

**key business drivers**

> The attributes of a business function that drive the behaviour and implementation of that business function in order to achieve the strategic business goals of the company.

**Key Performance Indicator**

> A measurable quantity against which specific Performance Criteria can be set when drawing up the SLA.

**Key Success Indicator**

> A measurement of success or maturity of a project or process.
>
> See also 'Critical Success Factor'.

**Knowledge Management**

> Discipline within an organisation that ensures that the intellectual capabilities of an organisation are shared, maintained and institutionalised.

**Known Error**

> An Incident or Problem for which the root cause is known and for which a temporary Work-around or a permanent alternative has been identified. If a business case exists, an RFC will be raised, but, in any event, it remains a Known Error unless it is permanently fixed by a change.

**latency**

> The elapsed time from the moment when a seek was completed on a disk device to the point when the required data is positioned under the read/write heads. It is normally defined by manufacturers as being half the disk rotation time.

**lifecycle**

> A series of states, connected by allowable transitions. The lifecycle represents an approval process for Configuration Items, Problem Reports and Change documents.

**logical I/O**

> A read or write request by a program. That request may, or may not, necessitate a physical I/O. For example, on a read request the required record may already be in a memory buffer and therefore a physical I/O is not necessary.

**marginal cost**

> The cost of providing the service now, based upon the investment already made.

**maturity level/milestone**

> The degree to which BCM activities and processes have become standard business practice within an organisation.

**metric**

> Measurable element of a service process or function.

**Operational Costs**

> Those costs resulting from the day-to-day running of the IT services section, e.g. staff costs, hardware maintenance and electricity, and relating to repeating payments whose effects can be measured within a short time-frame, usually less than the 12-month financial year.

**Operational Level Agreement (OLA)**

> An internal agreement covering the delivery of services which support the IT organisation in their delivery of services.

**Operations**

> All activities and measures to enable and/or maintain the intended use of the ICT infrastructure.

**opportunity cost (or true cost)**

> The value of a benefit sacrificed in favour of an alternative course of action. That is the cost of using resources in a particular operation expressed in terms of forgoing the benefit that could be derived from the best alternative use of those resources.

**outsourcing**

> The process by which functions performed by the organisation are contracted out for operation, on the organisation's behalf, by third parties.

**overheads**

> The total of indirect materials, wages and expenses.

**Package Assembly/Disassembly Device (PAD)**

> A device that permits terminals, which do not have an interface suitable for direct connection to a packet switched network, to access such a network. A PAD converts data to/from packets and handles call set-up and addressing.

**page fault**

> A program interruption that occurs when a page that is marked 'not in real memory' is referred to by an active page.

**Paging**

> The I/O necessary to read and write to and from the paging disks: real (not virtual) memory is needed to process data. With insufficient real memory, the operating system writes old pages to disk, and reads new pages from disk, so that the required data and instructions are in real memory.

**PD0005**

> Alternative title for the BSI publication 'A Code of Practice for IT Service Management'.

**percentage utilisation**

> The amount of time that a hardware device is busy over a given period of time. For example, if the CPU is busy for 1800 seconds in a one-hour period, its utilisation is said to be 50%.

**Performance Criteria**

> The expected levels of achievement which are set within the SLA against specific Key Performance Indicators.

**phantom line error**

> A communications error reported by a computer system that is not detected by network monitoring equipment. It is often caused by changes to the circuits and network equipment (e.g. re-routing circuits at the physical level on a backbone network) while data communications is in progress.

**physical I/O**

> A read or write request from a program has necessitated a physical read or write operation on an I/O device.

**prime cost**

> The total cost of direct materials, direct labour and direct expenses. The term prime cost is commonly restricted to direct production costs only and so does not customarily include direct costs of marketing or research and development.

**PRINCE2**

> The standard UK government method for project management.

**priority**

> Sequence in which an Incident or Problem needs to be resolved, based on impact and urgency.

**Problem**

> Unknown underlying cause of one or more Incidents.

**Problem Management**

> Process that minimises the effect on Customer(s) of defects in services and within the infrastructure, human errors and external events.

**process**

> A connected series of actions, activities, changes etc., performed by agents with the intent of satisfying a purpose or achieving a goal.

**Process Control**

> The process of planning and regulating, with the objective of performing the process in an effective and efficient way.

**programme**

> A collection of activities and projects that collectively implement a new corporate requirement or function.

**provider**

> The organisation concerned with the provision of IT services.

**Quality of Service**

> An agreed or contracted level of service between a service Customer and a Service Provider.

**queuing time**

> Queuing time is incurred when the device, which a program wishes to use, is already busy. The program therefore has to wait in a queue to obtain service from that device.

**RAID**

> Redundant Array of Inexpensive Disks – a mechanism for providing data resilience for computer systems using mirrored arrays of magnetic disks.

> Different levels of RAID can be applied to provide for greater resilience.

**reference data**

> Information that supports the plans and action lists, such as names and addresses or inventories, which is indexed within the plan.

**Release**

> A collection of new and/or changed CIs which are tested and introduced into the live environment together.

**remote fixes**

> Incidents or problems resolved without a member of the support staff visiting the physical location of the problems. Note: Fixing Incidents or problems remotely minimises the delay before the service is back to normal and are therefore usually cost-effective.

**Request For Change (RFC)**

Form, or screen, used to record details of a request for a change to any CI within an infrastructure or to procedures and items associated with the infrastructure.

**resolution**

Action which will resolve an Incident. This may be a Work-around.

**resource cost**

The amount of machine resource that a given task consumes. This resource is usually expressed in seconds for the CPU or the number of I/Os for a disk or tape device.

**resource profile**

The total resource costs that are consumed by an individual on-line transaction, batch job or program. It is usually expressed in terms of CPU seconds, number of I/Os and memory usage.

**resource unit costs**

Resource units may be calculated on a standard cost basis to identify the expected (standard) cost for using a particular resource. Because computer resources come in many shapes and forms, units have to be established by logical groupings. Examples are:

- CPU time or instructions
- disk I/Os
- print lines
- communication transactions.

**resources**

The IT services section needs to provide the Customers with the required services. The resources are typically computer and related equipment, software, facilities or organisational (people).

**Return On Investment**

The ratio of the cost of implementing a project, product or service and the savings as a result of completing the activity in terms of either internal savings, increased external revenue or a combination of the two. For instance, in simplistic terms if the internal cost of ICT cabling of office moves is £100,000 per annum and a structured cabling system can be installed for £300,000, then an ROI will be achieved after approximately three years.

**return to normal phase**

The phase within a business recovery plan which re-establishes normal operations.

**Risk**

A measure of the exposure to which an organisation may be subjected. This is a combination of the likelihood of a business disruption occurring and the possible loss that may result from such business disruption.

**Risk Analysis**

The identification and assessment of the level (measure) of the risks calculated from the assessed values of assets and the assessed levels of threats to, and vulnerabilities of, those assets.

**Risk Management**

The identification, selection and adoption of countermeasures justified by the identified risks to assets in terms of their potential impact upon services if failure occurs, and the reduction of those risks to an acceptable level.

**Risk reduction measure**

Measures taken to reduce the likelihood or consequences of a business disruption occurring (as opposed to planning to recover after a disruption).

**role**

A set of responsibilities, activities and authorisations.

**roll in, roll out (RIRO)**

Used on some systems to describe swapping.

**Rotational Position Sensing**

A facility which is employed on most mainframes and some minicomputers. When a seek has been initiated the system can free the path from a disk drive to a controller for use by another disk drive, while it is waiting for the required data to come under the read/write heads (latency). This facility usually improves the overall performance of the I/O subsystem.

**second-line support**

Where the fault cannot be resolved by first-line support or requires time to be resolved or local attendance.

**Security Management**

The process of managing a defined level of security on information and services.

**Security Manager**

The Security Manager is the role that is responsible for the Security Management process in the Service Provider organisation. The person is responsible for fulfilling the security demands as specified in the SLA, either directly or through delegation by the Service Level Manager. The Security Officer and the Security Manager work closely together.

**Security Officer**

The Security Officer is responsible for assessing the business risks and setting the security policy. As such, this role is the counterpart of the Security Manager and resides in the Customer's business organisation. The Security Officer and the Security Manager work closely together.

**seek time**

Occurs when the disk read/write heads are not positioned on the required track. It describes the elapsed time taken to move heads to the right track.

**segregation of duties**

Separation of the management or execution of certain duties or of areas of responsibility is required in order to prevent and reduce opportunities for unauthorised modification or misuse of data or service.

**self-insurance**

A decision to bear the losses that could result from a disruption to the business as opposed to taking insurance cover on the Risk.

**Service**

One or more IT systems which enable a business process.

**Service achievement**

The actual Service Levels delivered by the IT organisation to a Customer within a defined lifespan.

**Service Catalogue**

Written statement of IT services, default levels and options.

**Service Dependency Modelling**

Technique used to gain insight in the interdependency between an IT service and the Configuration Items that make up that service.

**Service Desk**

The single point of contact within the IT organisation for Users of IT services.

**Service Improvement Programme (SIP)**

A formal project undertaken within an organisation to identify and introduce measurable improvements within a specified work area or work process.

**Service Level**

The expression of an aspect of a service in definitive and quantifiable terms.

**Service Level Agreement (SLA)**

Written agreement between a Service Provider and the Customer(s) that documents agreed Service Levels for a service.

**Service Level Management (SLM)**

The process of defining, agreeing, documenting and managing the levels of Customer IT service, that are required and cost justified.

**Service Management**

Management of Services to meet the Customer's requirements.

**Service Provider**

Third-party organisation supplying services or products to Customers.

**Service quality plan**

The written plan and specification of internal targets designed to guarantee the agreed Service Levels.

**Service Request**

Every Incident not being a failure in the IT Infrastructure.

**Services**

The deliverables of the IT services organisation as perceived by the Customers; the services do not consist merely of making computer resources available for Customers to use.

**severity code**

Simple code assigned to problems and Known Errors, indicating the seriousness of their effect on the Quality of Service. It is the major means of assigning priority for resolution.

**simulation modelling**

Using a program to simulate computer processing by describing in detail the path of a job or transaction. It can give extremely accurate results. Unfortunately, it demands a great deal of time and effort from the modeller. It is most beneficial in extremely large or time-critical systems where the margin for error is very small.

**soft fault**

The situation in a virtual memory system when the operating system has detected that a page of code or data was due to be reused, i.e. it is on a list of 'free' pages, but it is still actually in memory. It is now rescued and put back into service.

**Software Configuration Item (SCI)**

As 'Configuration Item', excluding hardware and services.

**software environment**

Software used to support the application such as operating system, database management system, development tools, compilers, and application software.

**software library**

A controlled collection of SCIs designated to keep those with like status and type together and segregated from unlike, to aid in development, operation and maintenance.

**software work unit**

Software work is a generic term devised to represent a common base on which all calculations for workload usage and IT resource capacity are then based. A unit of software work for I/O type equipment equals the number of bytes transferred; and for central processors it is based on the product of power and CPU time.

**solid state devices**

Memory devices that are made to appear as if they are disk devices. The advantages of such devices are that the service times are much faster than real disks since there is no seek time or latency. The main disadvantage is that they are much more expensive.

**spec sheet**

Specifies in detail what the Customer wants (external) and what consequences this has for the Service Provider (internal) such as required resources and skills.

**stakeholder**

Any individual or group who has an interest, or 'stake', in the IT service organisation of a CSIP.

**standard cost**

A predetermined calculation of how many costs should be under specified working conditions. It is built up from an assessment of the value of cost elements and correlates technical specifications and the quantification of materials, labour and other costs to the prices and/or wages expected to apply during the period in which the standard cost is intended to be used. Its main purposes are to provide bases for control through variance accounting, for the valuation of work in progress and for fixing selling prices.

**standard costing**

A technique which uses standards for costs and revenues for the purposes of control through variance analysis.

**stand-by arrangements**

Arrangements to have available assets that have been identified as replacements should primary assets be unavailable following a business disruption. Typically, these include accommodation, IT systems and networks, telecommunications and sometimes people.

**storage occupancy**

A defined measurement unit that is used for storage type equipment to measure usage. The unit value equals the number of bytes stored.

**Strategic Alignment Objectives Model (SAOM)**

Relation diagram depicting the relation between a business function and its business drivers and the technology with the technology characteristics. The SAOM is a high-level tool that can help IT services organisations to align their SLAs, OLAs and acceptance criteria for new technology with the business value they deliver.

**Super User**

In some organisations it is common to use 'expert' Users (commonly known as Super or Expert Users) to deal with first-line support problems and queries. This is typically in specific application areas, or geographical locations, where there is not the requirement for full-time support staff. This valuable resource, however, needs to be carefully coordinated and utilised.

**surcharging**

Surcharging is charging business Users a premium rate for using resources at peak times.

**swapping**

The reaction of the operating system to insufficient real memory: swapping occurs when too many tasks are perceived to be competing for limited resources. It is the physical movement of an entire task (e.g. all real memory pages of an address space may be moved at one time from main storage to auxiliary storage).

**system**

An integrated composite that consists of one or more of the processes, hardware, software, facilities and people, that provides a capability to satisfy a stated need or objective.

**tension metrics**

A set of objectives for individual team members to use to balance conflicting roles and conflicting project and organisational objectives in order to create shared responsibility in teams and between teams.

**terminal emulation**

Software running on an intelligent device, typically a PC or workstation, which allows that device to function as an interactive terminal connected to a host system. Examples of such emulation software includes IBM 3270 BSC or SNA, ICL C03, or Digital VT100.

**terminal I/O**

A read from, or a write to, an on-line device such as a VDU or remote printer.

**third-line support**

Where specialists' skills (e.g. development/engineer) or contracted third-party support is required.

**third-party supplier**

An enterprise or group, external to the Customer's enterprise, which provides services and/or products to that Customer's enterprise.

**thrashing**

> A condition in a virtual storage system where an excessive proportion of CPU time is spent moving data between main and auxiliary storage.

**threat**

> An indication of an unwanted Incident that could impinge on the system in some way. Threats may be deliberate (e.g. wilful damage) or accidental (e.g. operator error).

**Total Cost of Ownership (TCO)**

> Calculated by including depreciation, maintenance, staff costs, accommodation, and planned renewal.

**tree structures**

> In data structures, a series of connected nodes without cycles. One node is termed the 'root' and is the starting point of all paths; other nodes termed 'leaves' terminate the paths.

**unabsorbed**

> overhead Any indirect cost that cannot be apportioned to a specific Customer.

**underpinning contract**

> A contract with an external supplier covering delivery of services that support the IT organisation in their delivery of services.

**unit costs**

> Costs distributed over individual component usage. For example, it can be assumed that, if a box of paper with 1000 sheets costs £10, then each sheet costs 1p. Similarly if a CPU costs £1m a year and it is used to process 1,000 jobs that year, each job costs on average £1,000.

**urgency**

> Measure of the business criticality of an Incident or Problem based on the impact and the business needs of the Customer.

**User**

> The person who uses the service on a day-to-day basis.

**Utility Cost Centre (UCC)**

> A cost centre for the provision of support services to other cost centres.

**variance analysis**

> A variance is the difference between planned, budgeted or standard cost and actual cost (or revenues). Variance analysis is an analysis of the factors that have caused the difference between the predetermined standards and the actual results. Variances can be developed specifically related to the operations carried out in addition to those mentioned above.

**version**

> An identified instance of a Configuration Item within a product breakdown structure or Configuration Structure for the purpose of tracking and auditing Change history. Also used for Software Configuration Items to define a specific identification released in development for drafting, review or modification, test or production.

**version identifier**

> A version number, version date, or version date and time stamp.

**virtual memory system**

A system that enhances the size of hard memory by adding an auxiliary storage layer residing on the hard disk.

**Virtual Storage Interrupt (VSI)**

An ICL VME term for a page fault.

**vulnerability**

A weakness of the system and its assets, which could be exploited by threats.

**warm stand-by**

See 'intermediate recovery'.

**waterline**

The lowest level of detail relevant to the Customer.

**Work-around**

Method of avoiding an Incident or Problem, either from a temporary fix or from a technique that means the Customer is not reliant on a particular aspect of the service that is known to have a Problem.

**workloads**

In the context of Capacity Management Modelling, a set of forecasts which detail the estimated resource usage over an agreed planning horizon. Workloads generally represent discrete business applications and can be further subdivided into types of work (interactive, timesharing, batch).

**WORM (Device)**

Optical read only disks, standing for Write Once Read Many.

**XML**

Extensible Markup Language. XML is a set of rules for designing text formats that let you structure your data. XML makes it easy for a computer to generate data, read data, and ensure that the data structure is unambiguous. XML avoids common pitfalls in language design: it is extensible, platform-independent, and it supports internationalisation and localisation.

# APPENDIX B DESIGN GUIDELINES TABLE

*Examples of a few design guidelines*

| | |
|---|---|
| Embedded application instrumentation | To be able to easily instrument distributed applications in a manner that allows support personnel to manage proactively a deployed application. Instrumentation enables applications to communicate their health and execution paths to support personnel. In order to make this instrumentation as useful as possible, it must meet the following requirements: |

- **Structured** – The data delivered within the instrumentation must be structured so that support personnel can automate repetitive support tasks.

- **Consistency** – A result of centralising the support of multiple business systems is that each system or even part of the system might report events in a different fashion. Bringing consistency to the events generated from the business systems allows the support personnel to automate redundant, error-prone support tasks.

- **Extensible** – An organisation will have a core set of events that define common event properties for all events as well as events for common scenarios. However, specific systems might need to extend the base event classes in order to communicate properly their administration events.

- **Minimally intrusive** – Adding instrumentation to an application must result in minimum overhead. For events that occur frequently, the delivery of the event must be fast and scalable. Frequent events must also have granular filtering whereby the administrator should be able to specify which categories of events should be delivered as well as what type of information should be added to the event.

- **Environment information** – A critical event must contain as much information as possible about the context of its event source.

- **Third party integration** – Events need to be made available to third party and legacy management tools.

- **Business Context** – When an event is emitted from a business system, a support person should be able to easily map the event to the business process that is affected by the event. This is crucial for understanding the severity of an event as it pertains to the organisation's business.

| | |
|---|---|
| Consistent exception processing | A number of systems deal with exceptions using a technique called structured exception handling. Structured exception handling is a mechanism used to make code more reliable by catching errors even if the programmer forgets to check error codes. It also makes it easier to write and maintain as the programmer isolates error handling rather than checking every error code. A procedure call can provide a handler, |

who describes what to do when an exception occurs. For instance, an application might catch and handle the error that would occur if the User tried to write to a diskette when the door was open. The exception handler would put a dialogue box up and prompt the User to close the door.

| | |
|---|---|
| Event monitoring/application health monitoring | Event management entails monitoring the health and status of enterprise systems, usually in real time, alerting administrators to problems, and consolidating the monitoring data in a single place for ease of administration. Event monitoring goes hand in hand with application instrumentation in that the instrumentation usually provides the events and information that the event monitoring system would consume to report on the state of the application. |
| Automated recovery using built-in redundancy, e.g. use of cluster arrangements | Having a number of pre-defined guidelines for dealing with the availability of an application helps application designers address non-functional requirements in a consistent manner across all applications. Special programming interfaces can be used to gain access to the platform's availability features, enabling the application designer to take advantage of recovery mechanisms, e.g. through the use of cluster arrangements. |

# APPENDIX C SERVICE DEPENDENCY MODELLING (SDM)

Chapter 7 describes the process of Service Dependency Modelling. This appendix adds some background information on how to build Service Dependency Models.

When completing a Service Dependency Model, each of the applications, layers, and interfaces need to be identified and documented as well as the expected operational behaviour and failure scenarios. The application behaviour and failure scenarios are normally documented in pseudo-code, which is an informal, English-like language developed for expressing algorithms normally converted later on into computer code for execution.

Pseudo-code is used to express the logic of the solution, and consists solely of executable statements. These statements are written in simple, structured English, not code, as shown in Figure C.1.

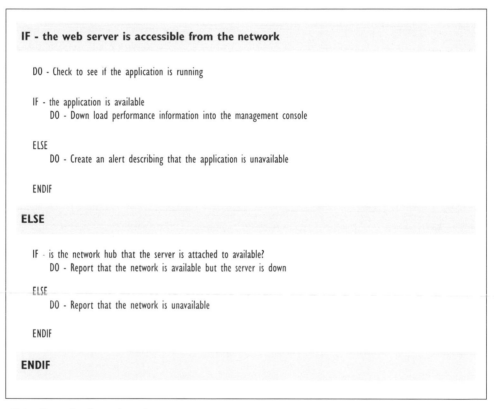

*Figure C.1 – Example of pseudo-code*

These layers would include how each of the applications talks to each other when looking at specific usage scenarios. An example of this could include a Customer placing an order on the website. The order would be stored in the database, and a database-stored procedure would then trigger an e-mail to be sent to a supplier to order the goods.

To identify and measure the contribution of an application to a Service Level, one needs to understand how the application affects each identifiable function within the SLA. Examples of this could be the response time of a Customer entry screen to get information back and update the screen following the placement of an order. The SLA defines the response time of less than five seconds for 99.9% of Customer transactions. The application relies on a browser, web server, host-based scripts, database server, stored procedures, and the underlying end-to-end infrastructure to deliver this SLA. In delivering this SLA, it is clear that each of these applications makes a critical contribution to the system meeting the SLA and failure of any of them would affect the SLA for some or all clients.

To start Service Dependency Modelling on a system, the following activities would normally be completed:

1   Identify the critical functionality that the system must deliver to meet its SLA.

2   Identify the applications that deliver each function and build a cross-reference table listing system functions against application features.

3   Identify application behaviour per system function that demonstrates that the system is correctly functioning, and add these to the application operation test table.

4   Identify application behaviour per system function that identifies failure scenarios and add these to the application failure test table.

5   Using the SLA for the system, prioritise operational and failure tests and build the pseudo-code (logic) necessary to build a Service Dependency Model for the application.

6   Create a graphic model that represents the Service Dependency Modelling, ideally in an enterprise Application Management tool.

7   Build the application test scripts out of the pseudo-code (logic) and incorporate these into the Service Dependency Model in the enterprise Application Management tool.

8   Test the Service Dependency Modelling to ensure that it matches and supports the SLA. This testing can be achieved by working through some of the usage scenarios under failure conditions.

**Tip**

**Good practice for the use of Service Dependency Modelling is to complete a full modelling exercise and then implement an automated Application Management tool to monitor the system behaviour. The results from this monitoring operation can then feed problems into the Service Desk's Incident Management system.**

# APPENDIX D QUALITY

### D.1     Quality Management

Quality Management for IT services is a systematic way of ensuring that all the activities necessary to design, develop and implement IT services which satisfy the requirements of the organisation and of users take place as planned and that the activities are carried out cost-effectively.

The way that an organisation plans to manage its Operations so that it delivers quality services is specified by its Quality Management System. The Quality Management System defines the organisational structure, responsibilities, policies, procedures, processes, standards and resources required to deliver quality IT services. However, a Quality Management System will only function as intended if management and staff are committed to achieving its objectives.

This appendix gives brief details on a number of different Quality approaches – more detail on these and other approaches can be found on the Internet at www.dti.gov.uk/quality.

### D.1.1     Deming

**Quote**

'We have learned to live in a world of mistakes and defective products as if they were necessary to life. It is time to adopt a new philosophy...'

(W. Edwards Deming, 1900–1993)

W. Edwards Deming is best known for his management philosophy for establishing quality, productivity, and competitive position. As part of this philosophy, he formulated 14 points of attention for managers. Some of these points are more appropriate to Service Management than others.

For quality improvement Deming proposed the Deming Cycle or Circle. The four key stages are 'Plan, Do, Check and Act' after which a phase of consolidation prevents the 'Circle' from 'rolling down the hill' as illustrated in Figure D.1.

The cycle is underpinned by a process led approach to management where defined processes are in place, the activities measured for compliance to expected values and outputs audited to validate and improve the process.

**Example**

Excerpts from Deming's 14 points relevant to Service Management

- break down barriers between departments (improves communications and management)

- management must learn their responsibilities, and take on leadership (process improvement requires commitment from the top; good leaders motivate people to improve themselves and therefore the image of the organisation)

- improve constantly (a central theme for service managers is continual improvement; this is also a theme for Quality Management. A process led approach is key to achieve this target)

- institute a programme of education and self-improvement (learning and improving skills have been the focus of Service Management for many years)

- training on the job (linked to continual improvement)

- transformation is everyone's job (the emphasis being on teamwork and understanding).

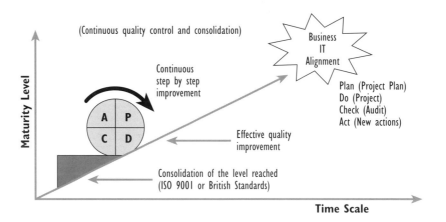

*Figure D.1 – The Deming Cycle*

### D.1.2 Juran

Joseph Juran became a recognised name in the quality field in 1951 with the publication of the Quality Control Handbook. The appeal was to the Japanese initially, and Juran was asked to give a series of lectures in 1954 on planning, organisational issues, management responsibility for Quality, and the need to set goals and targets for improvement.

Juran devised a well-known chart, 'The Juran Trilogy', shown in Figure D.2, to represent the relationship between quality planning, quality control, and quality improvement on a project-by-project basis.

A further feature of Juran's approach is the recognition of the need to guide managers; this is achieved by the establishment of a quality council within an organisation, which is responsible for establishing processes, nominating projects, assigning teams, making improvements and providing the necessary resources.

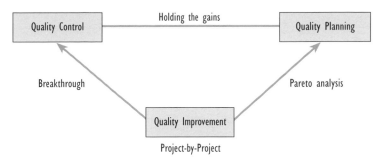

*Figure D.2 – The Quality trilogy*

Senior management plays a key role in serving on the quality council, approving strategic goals, allocating resources, and reviewing progress.

Juran promotes a four-phased approach to quality improvement, namely:

- Start-up – creating the necessary organisational structures and infrastructure
- Test – in which concepts are tried out in pilot programmes and results evaluated
- Scale-up – in which the basic concepts are extended based on positive feedback
- Institutionalisation – at which point quality improvements are linked to the strategic business plan.

### D.1.3    Crosby

The Crosby TQM approach is very popular in the UK. However, despite its obvious success in the market, it has been subject to much criticism, primarily due to poor understanding, or a blinkered application of the approach in some organisations, using a limited definition of quality. The approach is based on Crosby's Four Absolutes of Quality Management, namely:

- Quality is conformance to requirement
- The system for causing quality is prevention and not appraisal
- The performance standard must be zero defects and not 'that's close enough'
- The measure of quality is the price of non-conformance and not indices.

The Crosby approach is often based on familiar slogans; however, organisations may experience difficulty in translating the quality messages into sustainable methods of quality improvement. Some organisations have found it difficult to integrate their quality initiatives, having placed their quality programme outside the mainstream management process.

Anecdotal evidence suggests that these pitfalls result in difficulties being experienced in sustaining active quality campaigns over a number of years in some organisations.

Crosby lacks the engineering rigour of Juran and significantly omits to design quality into the product or process, gearing the quality system towards a prevention-only policy. Furthermore, it fails to recognise that few organisations have appropriate management measures from which they can accurately ascertain the costs of non-conformance, and in some cases even the actual process costs!

### D.1.4    Six Sigma

This is commonly described as a body of knowledge required to implement a generic quantitative approach to improvement. Six Sigma is a data-driven approach to analysing the root causes of problems and solving them. It is business output driven in relation to customer specification and focuses on dramatically reducing process variation using Statistical Process Control (SPC) measures. A process that operates at Six Sigma allows only 3.40 defects per million parts of output.

The Six Sigma approach has evolved from experience in manufacturing, and is therefore not readily applied to human processes and perhaps other processes that are not immediately apparent. The approach relies on trained personnel capable of identifying processes that need improvement and who can act accordingly. It does not contain a systematic approach for identifying improvement opportunities or facilitate with prioritisation.

Six Sigma perhaps offers another path toward measurable improvement for CMM Level 3 organisations, but this alone may make it difficult to apply in the context of Service Management compared to software engineering.

There are research reservations on applying validation and measurement to process improvement and particularly in the application of SPC to non-manufacturing engineering processes. It has been found that a Goal, Question, Metric (GQM) approach provides suitable measures, rather than a statistical method. It is still somewhat a controversial area, and even the SW-CMM at the higher levels (4–5) has come in for some academic criticism in this area. However, there are indications that Six Sigma is being applied in the service sector and, with good Service Management support tools, tracking of incidents, etc., would allow this approach to be used for process improvement.

## D.2    Formal quality initiatives

### D.2.1    Quality standards

#### International Standards Organisation ISO 9000

An important set of International Standards for Quality Assurance is the ISO 9000 range, a set of five universal standards for a Quality Assurance system that is accepted around the world. At the turn of the millennium, 90 or so countries have adopted ISO 9000 as the cornerstone of their national standards. When a product or service is purchased from a company that is registered to the appropriate ISO 9000 standard, the purchaser has important assurances that the quality of what they will receive will be as expected.

The most comprehensive of the standards is ISO 9001. It applies to industries involved in the design, development, manufacturing, installation and servicing of products or services. The standards apply uniformly to companies in any industry and of any size.

The BSI Management Overview of IT Service Management is a modern update of the original document, PD0005, which was published in 1995. The Management Overview is a management level introduction to Service Management, and in fact can be used as an introduction to ITIL. This is also now supported by a formal standard, BS 15000 (Specification for IT Service Management). ITIL is in many countries the *de facto* standard and, with the help of BSI and ISO, it is hoped that a formal international standard based on ITIL will soon be in place. The BSI Standard and Management Overview cover the established ITIL Service Support and Service Delivery processes, as well as some additional topics such as implementing the processes.

### D.2.2    Total Quality Systems: EFQM

> **Quote**
>
> '...the battle for Quality is one of the prerequisites for the success of your companies and for our collective success.'
>
> (Jacques Delors, president of the European Commission, at the signing of the letter of intent in Brussels to establish EFQM on 15 September 1988.)

#### The EFQM Excellence Model

The European Foundation for Quality Management (EFQM) was founded in 1988 by the Presidents of 14 major European companies, with the endorsement of the European Commission. The present membership is in excess of 600 very well-respected organisations, ranging from major multinationals and important national companies to research institutes in prominent European universities.

EFQM provides an excellent model for those wishing to achieve business excellence in a programme of continual improvement.

#### EFQM mission statement

The mission statement is:

> To stimulate and assist organisations throughout Europe to participate in improvement activities leading ultimately to excellence in customer satisfaction, employee satisfaction, impact on society and business results; and to support the Managers of European organisations in accelerating the process of making Total Quality Management a decisive factor for achieving global competitive advantage.

#### Depiction of the EFQM Excellence Model

The EFQM Excellence Model consists of 9 criteria and 32 sub-criteria; it is illustrated in Figure D.3.

In the model there is explicit focus on the value to users of the 'Plan, Do, Check, Act' cycle to business operations (see Section D.1.1), and the need to relate everything that is done, and the measurements taken, to the goals of business policy and strategy.

#### Self-assessment and maturity: the EFQM maturity scale

One of the tools provided by EFQM is the self-assessment questionnaire. The self-assessment process allows the organisation to discern clearly its strengths and also any areas where improvements can be made. The questionnaire process culminates in planned improvement actions, which are then monitored for progress.

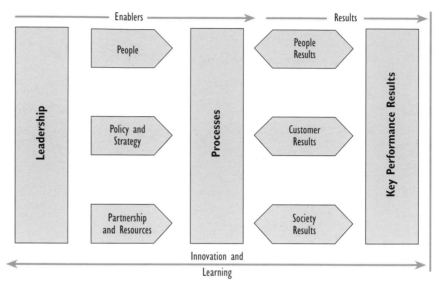

©EFQM. The EFQM Excellence Model is a registered trademark

*Figure D.3 – The EFQM Excellence Model*

In this assessment progress can be checked against a five-point maturity scale:

1  Product orientation

2  Process orientation (the maturity stage aimed for by the original ITIL)

3  System orientation (the maturity target for ITIL-compliant organisations in the new millennium)

4  Chain orientation

5  Total quality.

### D.2.3  Quality awards

To demonstrate a successful adaptation of the EFQM model, some companies aim for the European Quality Award, a process that allows Europe to recognise its most successful organisations and promote them as role models of excellence for others to copy.

The US equivalent to this award is the Malcolm Baldridge Quality Award for Quality Management. The Malcolm Baldridge National Quality Improvement Act of 1987 established an annual US National Quality Award. The purpose of the Award was (and still is) to promote awareness of quality excellence, to recognise quality achievements of US companies, and to publicise successful quality strategies.

For the Malcolm Baldridge Award, there are three categories:

■  Manufacturing companies or sub-units

■  Service companies or sub-units

■  Small businesses.

The criteria against which firms are judged are:

1  Leadership

2  Strategic planning

3 Customer and market focus

4 Information and analysis

5 Human resource development and management

6 Process management

7 Business results.

For the European Quality Award, there are four possible categories:

- Companies
- Operational units of companies
- Public sector organisations
- Small and medium enterprises.

The criteria against which candidate organisations are measured are:

1 Leadership

2 People

3 Policy and strategy

4 Partnerships and resources

5 Processes

6 People results

7 Customer results

8 Society results

9 Key performance results.

In the EFQM Excellence Model, the first four criteria are defined as enablers. Best practice in ITIL process implementations show that placing proper emphasis on these topics increases the chances for success. The key points for the four enablers are listed below.

### Leadership

- Organise a kick-off session involving everyone
- Be a role model
- Encourage and support the staff.

### People management

- Create awareness
- Recruit new staff and/or hire temporary staff to prevent Service Levels being affected during implementation stages
- Develop people through training and experience
- Align human resource plans with policy and strategy
- Adopt a coaching style of management
- Align performance with salaries.

## Policy and strategy

- Communicate mission, vision and values
- Align communication plans with the implementation stages.

## Partnerships and resources

- Establish partnerships with subcontractors and customers
- Use financial resources in support of policy and strategy
- Utilise existing assets.

# INDEX

# Other Information Sources and Services

## The IT Service Management Forum (itSMF)

The IT Service Management Forum Ltd (itSMF) is the only internationally recognised and independent body dedicated to IT Service Management. It is a not-for-profit organisation, wholly owned, and principally operated, by its membership.

The itSMF is a major influence on, and contributor to, Industry Best Practice and Standards worldwide, working in partnership with OGC (the owners of ITIL), the British Standards Institution (BSI), the Information Systems Examination Board (ISEB) and the Examination Institute of the Netherlands (EXIN).

Founded in the UK in 1991, there are now a number of chapters around the world with new ones seeking to join all the time. There are well in excess of 1000 organisations covering over 10,000 individuals represented in the membership. Organisations range from large multi-nationals such as AXA, GuinnessUDV, HP, Microsoft and Procter & Gamble in all market sectors, through central & local bodies, to independent consultants.

How to contact us:

The IT Service Management Forum Ltd
Webbs Court
8 Holmes Road
Earley
Reading RG6 7BH
Tel:     +44 (0) 118 926 0888
Fax:     +44 (0) 118 926 3073
Email:   service@itsmf.com
or visit our web-site at:
www.itsmf.com

## ITIL training and professional qualifications

There are currently two examining bodies offering equivalent qualifications: ISEB (The Information Systems Examining Board), part of the British Computer Society, and Stitching EXIN (The Netherlands Examinations Institute). Jointly with OGC and itSMF (the IT Service Management Forum), they work to ensure that a common standard is adopted for qualifications worldwide. The syllabus is based on the core elements of ITIL and complies with ISO9001 Quality Standard. Both ISEB and EXIN also accredit training organisations to deliver programmes leading to qualifications.

For further information:

visit ISEB's web-site at:
www.bcs.org.uk

and EXIN:
www.exin.nl